I0762507

THE POWER OF SHORT PRAYERS

THE POWER OF SHORT PRAYERS

JENTEZEN FRANKLIN

The Power of Short Prayers

ISBN: 978-1-963492-06-4
eBook: 978-1-963492-80-4
Audiobook: 978-1-963492-81-1

Produced by Breakfast for Seven
breakfastforseven.com

Printed in the United States of America.

TABLE OF CONTENTS

INTRODUCTION

"When you pray, don't ramble like heathens who think they'll be heard if they talk a lot."
(MATTHEW 6:7, GWT)

What Christian doesn't want to pray with more confidence and impact? To pray with more power. To move Heaven and earth when they come to the throne of grace for help in time of need. I know I do! When I intercede for myself, for my family, for my church, or for God's plans and purposes for the ministry, I want to know I'm opening Heaven's windows when I open my mouth.

I also know that it's easy to fall into the trap of thinking that longer prayers are better prayers. There is a temptation to believe the more we talk, the more persuasive we are in moving the hand of God. But that is not what the Bible shows us.

Your Bible is filled with examples of short prayers that brought breakthroughs, miracles, deliverance, and heavenly help. You'll find a collection of them on the pages that follow. In fact, you hold in your hands a guide to some of the shortest, yet most powerful, prayers in Scripture. Prayers for nearly every circumstance and season of life.

Your Bible declares: *"The effective, fervent prayer of a righteous man avails much"* (James 5:16). Please notice that it does not say, "the long, eloquent prayer..."

You can get a lot done with a short prayer. Let me give you a few reasons why.

For one thing, short prayers often carry a sense of urgency that long prayers don't. I've watched the mother of a toddler running out into a busy street shout the name "Jesus!" and then witnessed every car miraculously swerve or come to a sudden stop. That one-word prayer is as effective as the tongues of men and angels.

As we'll see in Chapter 5, Peter's short prayer, *"Lord, save me!"* in Matthew 14:30 (NIV), was enough to bring Jesus to his side when he was sinking.

Secondly, short prayers are powerful because the Bible says that when we pray, even briefly, God moves. Now that phrase, "God moves," may prompt a question in your mind. "Isn't God omnipresent? In what sense does He move? Isn't He everywhere, all the time?"

The answer is "Yes, of course." But when you pray, God, in a sense, "moves" from where He is to where you are. After all, doesn't the Word say, *"Draw near to God, and He will draw near to you,"* in James 4:8 (ESV)? Crying out to God in prayer is the best way to "draw near" to your heavenly Father.

You never know who God will call to do the impossible. Or when He will call upon you to partner with Him in bringing about a miracle. God can fix anything if we'll just pray. God is committed to restoring His creation, unwilling to leave it in a state of brokenness or abandonment. With divine wisdom, He knows how to mend what is broken. When you pray, He responds, accomplishing what is beyond your ability.

What is impossible with man is possible with God.

God's ears are ever and always inclined to the voices of His people. In the Gospels, we see that Jesus was frequently stopped by cries for help while on a journey to a specific place. Over and over, He stopped and brought about a miracle in response to those cries.

You may only see where you are right now, but God sees the glorious possibility of where you could be. You see where your loved one is right now, but God sees what is possible for them. In other words, just as Jesus demonstrated, God will pause His *purpose* to bring about your *possibility*.

I hope that as we look at each prayer together, you'll feel encouraged that God is kind and loves to answer the prayers of His people, making your faith stronger. And that as you read each entry, you'll find ways to apply to your own life and circumstances the truth and principles they contain.

Please don't misunderstand, though. I'm not suggesting that you spend less time talking to God. Fellowship with Him. Pour out your heart to Him. Spend all the time you can in intimate connection with Him. By all means, carve out as much time as you can to quiet your soul and listen for His voice of wisdom. Just don't make the mistake Jesus pointed to in the verse at the start of this introduction. Here is that same verse in the more-familiar New King James translation:

> *"And when you pray, do not use vain repetitions as the heathen do. For they think that they will be heard for their many words."* (Matthew 6:7)

Longer isn't necessarily better. Sometimes less is more. Get ready to discover the power of short prayers!

Short prayers are *powerful* because the Bible says that when we pray, even briefly, *God moves*.

CHAPTER 1

When You're Facing a Huge Obstacle or Impossible Situation

A 2-Word Prayer

This is the word of the Lord *to Zerubbabel: "Not by might nor by power, but by My Spirit," says the* Lord *of hosts. "Who are you, O great mountain? Before Zerubbabel you shall become a plain! And he shall bring forth the capstone with shouts of* ***'Grace, grace*** *to it!'"*

(ZECHARIAH 4:6–7, EMPHASIS ADDED)

I have a confession for you. I talk to mountains. I do it all the time. And here is another revelation that might startle you. When I talk to mountains, they hear me. I'll start with giving you a little context for the Scripture passage above.

After the Jews were released from 70 years in captivity in Babylon and allowed to return home to Judah, they found Jerusalem in ruins. By the time a remnant returned home, the once-magnificent Temple of Solomon that had previously shone in blinding white and gold at the summit of Mount Zion had been a charred pile of rubble for seven decades. Its sacred stones, a habitat for wild animals and nomads.

Zerubbabel, the leader of the returning remnant, had been sent back by God to rebuild, restore, and restart the city of Jerusalem and to resurrect Solomon's Temple. If you read the entire passage, you discover that he started trying to rebuild the temple first, but things weren't going well. In fact, he spent years trying to organize the project and got nowhere.

Zerubbabel was simply trying his best to do what God had called him to do but found himself running into one roadblock or obstacle after another. He was getting nowhere. Years of hard work and effort went by with no progress to show for it.

Then something strange happened. Zerubbabel had a vision.

An angel appeared to him and began to show him a series of images. And one of those images was of a mountain standing between himself and the fully rebuilt temple. Then the angel delivered a word from the Lord to Zerubbabel. Those words are in the key Scripture verses above.

First, "the Lord of Hosts" reminds Zerubbabel of an important truth. A truth that God does things differently than we do. And that if we're going to do things God's way, we'll be different, too. That reminder was:

"'Not by might nor by power, but by My Spirit,' says the Lord of hosts."

Oh, how I love this truth! We tend to want to do things with *natural* strategies and *natural* tools in our own, *natural* strength. That's what poor, frustrated Zerubbabel had obviously been doing. But God delivered the truth. God gets things done, not by natural power and might, but with supernatural strategies, tools, and strength. *"'By My Spirit,' says the Lord of Hosts."*

Then after that amazing declaration, something even more shocking happens. God, through the angel, demonstrates what it looks like to do things the supernatural way. What did the messenger do?

He started talking to the mountain standing between Zerubbabel and his God-given goal.

I really like the way this angel shows Zerubbabel how to deal with a mountain-sized obstacle. He starts out by asking a pointed question: *"Who are you, O great mountain?"* In other words, "Identify yourself!" "Who do you think you are, daring to stand between me and what God has called me to do?"

This is immediately followed by a prophecy: *"Before Zerubbabel you shall become a plain!"* In other words, "You may look like a giant mountain obstacle now, but before my man Zerubbabel, you're about to become a flat highway." Then the Lord reveals *how* Zerubbabel is going to bring that about. So, what will flatten a mountain like a pancake?

"With shouts of, 'Grace, grace' to it!"

Isn't that amazing? Among all the short prayers of the Bible, this is one of the very shortest. And it is also one of the most powerful. The saying, "Faith can move mountains," is absolutely true. But now you know that yes, faith can *move* them, but grace can *flatten* them!

Note that the word grace is shouted, not once, but twice. This prayer is calling for a "double portion" of grace for removal of the obstacle.

Faith can move mountains, but grace can flatten them!

Grace is a special word from the Bible. It shows up over 100 times! There are four different types of grace in the Bible. When you see the word "grace" while reading, it's good to figure out which type it's talking about. Which one of these four types is Zerubbabel excited about here?

Sometimes the Scriptures are talking about "saving grace." This type of grace lies at the heart of one of the most well-known grace verses in the entire Bible:

> *For by grace you have been saved through faith, and that not of yourselves; it is the gift of God, not of works, lest anyone should boast.* (Ephesians 2:8–9)

The amazing truth of that iconic passage is that you can't earn or deserve salvation. It's declaring that you don't get good to get God. No, you get God in order to get good. Our walk of faith isn't working or deserving or meriting or earning our salvation. We're saved by grace, not by works. Salvation is not do, do, do. It's done, done, done—in and by Jesus. From the cross He cried out, *"It is finished!"* (John 19:30, NASB). And He meant it.

Our *walk of faith* isn't working or deserving or meriting or earning our salvation.

Just pause for a moment and thank your heavenly Father for that. We're saved not by our performance, but by what Jesus did on the cross. That's "saving grace." I thank God for it. But it is not the kind of grace that moves mountains out of your way.

There is another kind of grace. One that is often called *justifying* grace.

In the third chapter of Romans, right after declaring that *"all have sinned and fall short of the glory of God"* (v. 23), Paul makes this statement:

> *Being justified freely by His grace through the redemption that is in Christ Jesus.* (Romans 3:24)

Let's pull that little sentence apart. First we find, *"being justified freely."* Justification is a fancy theology word that simply means "just-as-if-I'd-never sinned." It describes a condition of being completely right with God. And the word "freely" means we don't earn that condition. It's a gift. A *freely* given gift. And how do we get that gift? "... *through the redemption that is in Christ Jesus."*

God's grace truly is amazing! When the accuser comes to attack us, it's God's grace that covers us and declares, "No. You stand just as if you'd never sinned because you've been justified freely by His grace!" Justifying grace is wonderful. But it is not the kind of grace that you shout at mountains about.

There is a third kind of grace evident in your Bible. It's called *teaching* grace. This is one that many believers aren't aware of. We find it mentioned in the second chapter of Titus:

> *For the grace of God that brings salvation has appeared to all men, <u>teaching us</u> that, denying ungodliness and worldly lusts, we should live soberly, righteously, and godly in the present age.* (Titus 2:11–12, emphasis added)

Notice that the grace of God has appeared doing what? *"Teaching us..."* What is it teaching us? Teaching us what? How to *"live soberly, righteously, and godly in the present age"* by *"denying ungodliness and worldly lusts."*

Isn't that amazing? Very few Christians understand that grace is connected with holiness. Some people seem to believe that the grace of God is permission to do wrong. To live without restraint. But clearly, that is not what grace is. These verses make it clear that grace will *teach* you how to live a holy life. That's a great thing. But this is not the form of grace that the angel in Zechariah is shouting about.

No, the kind of grace here is *enabling* grace.

Any kind of grace is amazing. I'll take any and all I can get! But enabling grace is especially wonderful. It is a supernatural gift of ability. A God-given gift of power to accomplish something you could never, ever accomplish in your own strength.

Do you recall Paul's mention of his "thorn in the flesh" in 2 Corinthians, chapter 12? Here's a reminder:

> *And lest I should be exalted above measure by the abundance of the revelations, a thorn in the flesh was given to me, a messenger of Satan to buffet me, lest I be exalted above measure. Concerning this thing* ***I pleaded with the Lord three times that it might depart from me.*** *And He said to me,* ***"My grace is sufficient for you, for My strength is made perfect in weakness."*** *Therefore most gladly I will rather boast in my infirmities, that the power of Christ may rest upon me.* (vv. 7–9, emphasis added)

The Greek word translated "strength" there is *dunamis*, often translated "power" in the New Testament—and literally means "enablement." That is, supernatural strength and power that *enables* you to do what you could never do in your own strength.

Paul was dealing with some sort of affliction or trouble. There is no point in speculating about what it was here. It doesn't matter. What matters is that Paul prayed three times for it to be removed but then heard a specific word from the Lord. God came back with this answer.

Grace! *"My grace is sufficient for you."*

Why was it sufficient? *"... for My strength* [power] *is made perfect in weakness."* In other words, God loves to give enabling grace in the midst of circumstances in which you have no natural strength or ability to get a breakthrough—that is, "your weakness."

In your Bible, whenever you see grace coupled with supernatural power, you know the kind of grace you're looking at is *enabling* grace. With Paul, God is declaring that His grace was going to *enable* Paul to endure and overcome.

When God said, *"My grace is sufficient for you,"* He was saying, "I'm not taking it away. I'm not taking you out of it. I'm going to allow you to go through this, but my grace will be sufficient for you to overcome it and come out the other side in victory." In other words, Paul took his thorn in the flesh to the throne of grace.

When you have enabling grace, you can do things that mere mortals can't do and deal with pressure that would wipe other people out.

Enabling grace is grace that "helps." This is why Hebrews 4:16 declares:

> *Let us therefore come boldly to the throne of grace, that we may obtain mercy and find* ***grace to help in time of need.***

That's enabling grace. That brings us back to Zerubbabel's vision of shouting "Grace! Grace!" to the mountain that stood between him and his holy calling and goal—to rebuild the temple of God.

Yes, he talked to his mountain. He began by saying, "Identify yourself! Who do you think you are, to stand between me and the job the Most High God has assigned me to do?" Instead of running to God to tell Him how big that mountain was, he ran to the mountain to tell it how big his God was!

The idea of talking to a mountain should make us think of Mark chapter eleven:

> *So Jesus answered and said to them, "Have faith in God. For assuredly, I say to you, whoever* ***says to this mountain, 'Be removed and be cast into the sea,'*** *and does not doubt in his heart, but believes that those things he says will be done, he will have whatever he says."* (vv. 22–23, emphasis added)

That's from the mouth of the Savior Himself. So perhaps we shouldn't think of speaking to mountains or obstacles as something strange.

I vividly recall the season of time decades ago when the church I pastor in Gainesville, Georgia was relatively young and we were building a new sanctuary.

We had scraped together enough money to buy eighteen acres of undeveloped land. We were so excited, but there was just one problem. It was basically a huge eighteen-acre mountain or hill. And you can't build on a hill. You need it to be flat.

That meant we were going to spend a lot of money up front doing what they call the "dirt work." The mountain needed to become a flat plain before we could build a church on it. So, in came all the big earth moving equipment to remove forty feet off the top of that mountain.

At that time our three girls—Courteney, Caressa, and Caroline—were all still little. Every day we'd drive by that acreage with the three little girls in the back seat and I'd reach my hand out to that property and shout "Grace! Grace!" to it.

Soon all three of the girls were doing it as well! We'd drive down that road and the moment we turned the corner I'd hear three little voices from three little car seats shouting "Grace! Grace!" with little hands stretched out toward that construction site.

What is your impossible need today? Whatever it is, that is your mountain.

Don't let that mountain do all the talking. Talk to it. Ask it who it thinks it is to stand between a child of God and your God-ordained destiny or His promises.

Come boldly to the throne of grace in faith to receive helping, enabling grace in your time of need. We serve the God who delights in giving enabling grace. As He told Zerubbabel, it is not by human might or human power that your mountain will be flattened. No, it is *"by My Spirit,"* says the Lord.

Don't let that mountain do all the talking.
Talk to it.

In this very moment, God is saying to you, "If I asked you to start it, I'm empowering you, by My grace, to finish it. I who began a good work in you will complete it! (Philippians 1:6). No obstacle standing between you and what I've called you to do can stand when you shout 'Grace! Grace!' to it. For I am ready, willing, and able to gift enabling grace to you in abundance."

No matter how tough a situation becomes, your obstacles do not have to become your tombstone. In fact, they can become your steppingstones into even greater blessings that God has prepared for you. Talk to your mountain.

Your Short Prayer:

Father, by Your enabling gift of power I speak "Grace! Grace!" to the mountain that stands between me and Your highest and best.

CHAPTER 2

When You or a Loved One Needs to "See" Spiritual Truth

A 10-Word Prayer

And Elisha prayed, and said, ***Lord, I pray thee, open his eyes, that he may see.*** *And the Lord opened the eyes of the young man; and he saw: and, behold, the mountain was full of horses and chariots of fire round about Elisha.*

(2 KINGS 6:17, KJV)

Sometimes we find ourselves in desperate need for God to "open the eyes" of someone we love. I'm talking about *spiritual* eyes. I mean when you or someone you care about seems blind to something that seems obvious to you. And that blindness is putting them in danger.

It might be a son or daughter who has wandered away from the faith. It might be a spouse who wants out of the marriage. It might be a longtime friend who is headed down a dark path.

Only God can open the eyes of a loved one to spiritual truth and realities. But, other times the person who needs better spiritual vision is us!

In either case, Elisha's simple, ten-word prayer found in 2 Kings 6, and the circumstances around it, offer you and me some important encouragement.

Only God can open the eyes of a loved one to *spiritual truth* and *realities*.

Let's begin by setting the scene for that prayer. Here's the scriptural context:

> *Now the king of Syria was making war against Israel... Therefore he sent horses and chariots and a great army there, and they came by night and surrounded the city. And when the servant of the man of God [Elisha] arose early and went out, there was an army, surrounding the city with horses and chariots. And his servant said to him, "Alas, my master! What shall we do?"*
> (vv. 8, 14–15)

Elisha—the prophet of God and protégé of Elijah—is living in the city of Dothan in the northern kingdom of Israel. The ruler of Syria has been hoping for some time to attack and capture Israel's king, but Elisha has been using his prophetic gifting to help the king escape capture.

The Syrian king is frustrated and angry. He can't figure out why Israel's king always avoids his traps. His prey always seems one step ahead of him. In fact, he's beginning to think he has a traitor in his inner circle. He doesn't know that Israel's king doesn't need a spy in the Syrian camp.

He has something far better: a prophet of the Most High God, the One who sees all and knows all.

After yet another failure to capture the king of Israel, the enraged Syrian king asks his advisors, *"Will you not show me which of us is for the king of Israel?"* (v. 11). In other words, "which one of you guys is secretly playing for the other team?"

One of those advisors actually knows the truth and says, *"None, my lord, O king; but Elisha, the prophet who is in Israel, tells the king of Israel the words that you speak in your bedroom"* (v. 12).

So now the Syrian king knows who to go after. Elisha is his problem. Such a problem, in fact, that he probably knows what the king is saying in his private bed chambers. Clearly, Elisha has to be eliminated. And soon the king learns exactly where he is.

On a morning not too many days later, Elisha's servant gets up early in the morning. But looking around, he sees the entire village surrounded by a vast army of Syrian soldiers and horse-drawn chariots.

In a panic, the servant yells for Elisha and shouts, *"This is hopeless, my master! What are we to do?"* (v. 15, NASB). They were in a pickle. Actually, that's a huge understatement. They were in an impossible situation!

Have you ever felt completely surrounded by impossible circumstances, unable to see any way out?

Maybe it was a financial crisis that seemed insurmountable, with bills piling up and no relief in sight. Perhaps it was a relationship that appeared beyond repair or a health diagnosis that felt like a death sentence. It could have been watching a loved one spiral into addiction, wondering if they'd ever find their way back to God.

If so, you understand exactly what Elisha's servant was experiencing when he ran into the house in panic, crying, *"What are we to do?"*

In moments like that, you and the people you love need what Elisha's servant needed. You see, Elisha wasn't at all troubled by the situation. In fact, Elisha said, *"Do not fear, for those who are with us are more than those who are with them"* (v. 16).

That servant at first must have thought his boss wasn't fully awake yet. "Surely, he's not understanding the situation we're in. Maybe he's really, really bad at math. Or maybe he's not seeing well this morning."

"*Do not fear*, for those who are with us are more than those who are with them."

In reality, it was the servant who had a "seeing" problem. Here's Elisha's ten-word prayer that changed everything: *"Lord, I pray, open his eyes, that he may see"* (v. 17).

As an anointed prophet, Elisha was accustomed to seeing what is going on in the unseen realm of the spirit. There are always things going on around us that can't be perceived with our five natural senses. But the realm of the spirit—where angels and demons move and work—is just as real as the natural realm. (Perhaps even more so.)

This helps us understand why Elisha wasn't at all flustered by the appearance of the Syrian army on his doorstep. Here was Heaven's response to that ten-word prayer:

> *Then the Lord opened the eyes of the young man, and he saw. And behold, the mountain was full of horses and chariots of fire all around Elisha.* (v. 17)

At first, all the servant could see was what his natural sight could show him. And what it showed him was terrifying. But in response to Elisha's request, his servant was granted the ability to "see" supernatural realities in addition to natural realities.

And what he saw was he and Elisha encircled by heavenly horses and flaming chariots. Heaven had dispatched overwhelming firepower to protect the man of God. The Word doesn't say so, but I suspect that as soon as the servant got over the shock of the sight, he grew as calm and collected as his master.

Moments earlier, two men were facing identical circumstances. Yet one was panicking and the other was calm and confident. What was the difference? Sight! Spiritual sight.

This story teaches us something crucial about the difference between natural sight and spiritual vision. The Syrian army was real—the servant could see them with his natural eyes, count their weapons, and assess their strength. But what he couldn't see with natural vision was the supernatural protection that surrounded them. God's army of angels had been there the entire time, invisible to human sight but more real and more powerful than any earthly force.

Elisha's prayer demonstrates that sometimes the most powerful thing we can do for someone who is overwhelmed by circumstances is to ask God to open their eyes to spiritual reality. The servant didn't need the circumstances to change—he needed to see the circumstances from God's perspective.

This principle extends far beyond ancient battlefields. In our modern world, we're constantly bombarded with messages that tell us to trust only what we can see, measure, and verify with our physical senses. We're taught to base our decisions on visible evidence, statistical analysis, and logical reasoning. While these tools have their place, they can also blind us to spiritual realities that are more powerful than anything we can see with our natural eyes.

When we're facing overwhelming challenges, our tendency is to focus entirely on what we can see: the size of the problem, the strength of the opposition, or the limited resources at our disposal. We count the enemy forces and measure our own strength, and often conclude that we're hopelessly outnumbered.

But Elisha's ten-word prayer reminds us that there's always more to the story than what meets the eye. The same God who surrounded Elisha with chariots of fire surrounds you with His protection today. The same angelic forces that were ready to defend the prophet are available to you as His child.

The same God who surrounded Elisha with chariots of fire *surrounds you* with His protection today.

Sometimes we need to pray Elisha's prayer for ourselves: "Lord, open my eyes to see the spiritual reality of my situation." Other times, like Elisha, we need to pray it for someone we love who is overwhelmed by what they're facing.

Let me share two other powerful examples from Scripture where God opened people's eyes to see beyond their natural circumstances.

The first involves a desperate mother named Hagar and her son Ishmael. As we see in the twenty-first chapter of Genesis, after being cast out of Abraham's household, the two found themselves dying of thirst in the desert. Hagar had given up hope and placed her son under a bush. She simply couldn't bear to watch him die. She sat down at a distance and wept, believing there was no help available.

But God heard the voice of the boy crying out, and an angel appeared with a message of hope: *"Fear not, for God has heard the voice of the lad where he is"* (v. 17). Then comes this beautiful phrase: *"Then God opened her eyes, and she saw a well of water"* (v. 19).

The well had been there all along. The provision Hagar needed was within reach, but she couldn't see it until God opened her eyes. How often do we find ourselves in similar situations—surrounded by God's provision but unable to see it because we're focused on our circumstances rather than His resources?

This story carries a special message for parents whose children have wandered away from God. Just as God heard Ishmael's cry in the desert, He hears the voice of your child wherever they are. The prayers you prayed over them, the scriptures you taught them, the foundation you laid in their lives—all of that creates a voice within them that cries out to God even when they're far from Him.

You may not be able to see your prodigal child's spiritual condition clearly, but God can. When He opens your eyes, you'll see that His hand is still on their life, that His plan for them is still good, and that the well of His grace is available even in their desert season.

Another example involves the prophet Balaam. As we see in Numbers chapter twenty-two, Balaam was traveling down the wrong road for the wrong reasons. He had been bribed by a pagan to curse God's people, and as he rode his donkey toward his destination, the Angel of the Lord with a drawn sword appeared in the road to stop him.

The remarkable thing about this story is that the donkey could see the Angel, but the prophet couldn't. Every time the donkey tried to avoid the Angel, Balaam beat the animal for not staying on the path. The donkey was actually trying to save Balaam's life, but the prophet was so focused on his own agenda that he couldn't see the spiritual reality of his situation. What happened next?

> *Then the* Lord *opened Balaam's eyes, and he saw the Angel of the* Lord *standing in the way with His drawn sword in His hand; and he bowed his head and fell flat on his face.* (v. 31)

Do you see it? The "Lord opened Balaam's eyes!" And he saw the angel that had been blocking his path. He realized that what he thought was an obstruction to his plans was actually God's protection from destruction.

How often do we find ourselves in Balaam's position—frustrated because we can't seem to make progress in a direction we want to go, not realizing that God is protecting us from disaster? Sometimes what we perceive as God fighting against us is actually God fighting for us.

When God opens our eyes, we can see that the detours, delays, and apparent obstacles in our lives may actually be His way of steering us away from danger and toward His perfect plan. The relationship that didn't work out, the job that fell through, the opportunity that never materialized—these may have been God's protection rather than His rejection.

When God *opens our eyes*, we can see that the detours, delays, and apparent obstacles in our lives may actually be His way of steering us away from danger and toward His *perfect plan*.

The phrase "God opened their eyes" appears four times in Scripture, and each time it reveals something crucial about spiritual sight:

First, when God opens your eyes, you can see provision that was there all along. Like Hagar discovering the well in the desert, you'll recognize that God's resources have been available even when you couldn't see them.

Second, when God opens your eyes, you can see the right direction when you've been going the wrong way. Like Balaam seeing the Angel with the drawn sword, you'll understand that what seemed like obstruction was actually protection.

Third, when God opens your eyes, you can see the protection that surrounds you. Like Elisha's servant seeing the chariots of fire, you'll realize that God's forces are greater than any opposition you face.

Fourth, when God opens your eyes, you can see that Jesus was there all along, even when you didn't recognize Him. Like the disciples on the road to Emmaus, you'll realize that Christ was present in your situation even when you felt most alone.

These principles have profound implications for how we pray and how we view our circumstances. Instead of asking God to change our situations, sometimes we need to ask Him to change our perspective. Instead of pleading for Him to remove the obstacles, we might need to pray for eyes to see how He's working through them.

Elisha's ten-word prayer is particularly powerful because it recognizes that the real battle is often not in the physical realm but in the spiritual realm. The servant didn't need a bigger army or better weapons—he needed supernatural sight to see that God had already provided everything necessary for victory.

This same principle applies to many of the battles we face today. When you're dealing with financial pressure, the real battle isn't just about money—it's about trusting that God knows your needs and has provision available. When you're facing health challenges, the real battle isn't just physical—it's about believing that God's healing power is greater than any diagnosis. When you're worried about your children, the real battle isn't just about their choices—it's about having faith that God's grace is pursuing them even when they're far from Him.

The enemy wants to keep your eyes focused on the visible circumstances because he knows that what you see determines how you feel, and how you feel often determines how you act. If you can only see the problems, you'll be paralyzed by fear. If you can only see the obstacles, you'll be tempted to give up. If you can only see the opposition, you'll feel overwhelmed and defeated.

But when God opens your eyes to spiritual reality, everything changes. You'll see that the same God who parted the Red Sea, who brought down the walls of Jericho, and who raised Jesus from the dead is actively working in your situation. You'll realize that the forces fighting for you are greater than the forces fighting against you.

Sometimes we need to pray Elisha's prayer for ourselves: "Lord, open my eyes to see Your provision, Your protection, and Your presence in my situation." Other times we need to pray it for family members who are overwhelmed by their circumstances: "Lord, open their eyes to see that You're still in control, that You still have a plan, and that they're not fighting this battle alone."

This prayer is especially powerful for parents whose children are struggling. When you can't see any evidence that God is working in your child's life, ask Him to open your eyes to the spiritual reality. That foundation you laid through years of prayer and teaching is still there. God is still hearing the voice of your child even when they're far from Him. His plan for their life is still good, even when their current choices are destructive.

The same God who opened the eyes of Elisha's servant is available to open your eyes today. He wants you to see beyond the temporary circumstances to the eternal realities. He wants you to understand that His army surrounds you, His provision is available to you, and His presence is with you even when you can't feel it.

When you're facing your own impossible situation, remember Elisha's confidence: "Those who are with us are more than those who are with them." Then pray his ten-word prayer and ask God to give you supernatural sight to see what He sees.

The chariots of fire are still there. The angels are still encamped around those who fear the Lord. The well of God's provision is still available in every desert season. God's protection is still surrounding you and your loved ones.

You don't always need your circumstances to change—sometimes you just need your eyes to be opened to see the spiritual reality of your situation.

Your Short Prayer:

Lord, I pray, open my eyes that I may see. Help me and my loved one see beyond our circumstances and to Your spiritual reality. Show us Your provision, Your protection, and Your presence in this situation.

CHAPTER 3

When You Need Healing Mercies

A 6-Word Prayer

Then as He entered a certain village, there met Him ten men who were lepers, who stood afar off. And they lifted up their voices and said, ***"Jesus, Master, have mercy on us!"***
(LUKE 17:12–13)

"Jesus, Master, have mercy on us!*" These six words, spoken from the depths of unimaginable desperation, became a doorway to supernatural healing and release from a living hell.

Mercy. The mercy of God! It's not just pitiful lepers who need it. We're all in desperate need of it. But never more so than when we get bad news at the doctor's office. So here is wonderful news. Your heavenly Father's supplies of mercy are inexhaustible. In fact, according to Lamentations 3:23, they are *"new every morning."*

Charles Spurgeon said it this way: "God's mercy is so great that you may sooner drain the sea of its water, or deprive the sun of its light... than diminish the great mercy of God."[1]

The nineteenth-century preacher A.B. Simpson once wrote, "The mercy of God is an ocean divine, a boundless and fathomless flood. Launch out in the deep, cut away the shoreline, and be lost in the mercy of God."[2]

The mercy of our Savior was on full display in this beautiful story from Luke, chapter seventeen. It reminds us that sometimes our simplest prayers carry the most profound power—not because of their eloquence, but because they appeal in desperate faith to the compassionate heart of a heavenly Father.

Imagine yourself there with Jesus, somewhere between Samaria and Galilee, as the Redeemer spots ten skeletal figures dressed in rags staggering and stumbling toward him.

Sometimes *our simplest prayers* carry the *most profound power*—not because of their eloquence, but because they appeal in desperate faith to the compassionate heart of a heavenly Father.

Before we go deeper into this amazing moment and what it means for us, let's first get a clear picture of how awful leprosy was. We'll also look at what leprosy stands for in the Bible. Once you understand that, you'll see why this short prayer is so powerful.

Leprosy is a contagious disease caused by a certain type of bacteria. Today it is curable, but, in Jesus' day, someone infected with the disease faced a long, terrible, lonely death.

There was no cure. And if a person with leprosy dared to enter the marketplace or any place where people gathered, he or she risked being stoned. Religious and civil law required a leper to stay far away from any other person. And if, for some reason, you needed to pass through an area where people were, you were required to shout from afar off, "Unclean! Unclean!" This gave people a chance to clear out and avoid you.

Although the disease can damage the eyes, weaken the muscles, and compromise the immune system, the primary effect is nerve damage in the areas to which it has spread throughout the body. This nerve damage destroyed the ability to feel pain. This in turn led to the loss of body parts—fingers, toes, hands, feet, nose, lips, and ears—through repeated injuries and the infections that fester in those unnoticed wounds.

The first sign of the disease would begin with a little pink, numb spot somewhere on the skin. Then the spots would begin to spread throughout the body and become increasingly inflamed.

And after it would spread, any sores would fester, ulcerate, and then begin to drain. At that point a terrible stench would develop. As the disease would spread all over the body, the hair of the victim would fall out. Even the eyebrows would fall off. Often, leprosy would cause the nose and lips to waste away, turning a once-familiar face into something frightening.

As horrific as this sounds, none of these miseries were the saddest effect of leprosy in that day. No, the worst aspect of all was likely the isolation. We humans are social creatures. God designed us to live in families and in communities. Yet leprosy resulted in a total loss of contact with family, friends, neighbors, and coworkers. Because of its contagious nature, an appearance of leprosy on a person meant being cast out of the community.

Yes, the long, slow death sentence of the disease itself also sentenced the sufferer to a lonely life on the fringes of society. This isolation was especially enforced in ancient Jewish communities because Mosaic law designated a leper as ceremonially defiled or "unclean."

Imagine never being able to touch another human being again. Imagine knowing you would never again feel the touch of your child's hand or the goodnight kiss of your spouse. Or even the hug of a dear, old friend. Your days of human contact were over the moment you were diagnosed. It was forbidden by the strictest laws and regulations imaginable. Few if any people would ever dare to touch you even if the laws permitted it.

These ten desperate lepers who dared to approach Jesus weren't just individuals dealing with illness—they were souls like you and me, experiencing the deepest form of isolation our human hearts can know. Leprosy began as something small, almost unnoticeable, before gradually overtaking every aspect of their existence. The physical manifestations—inflammation, sores, loss of sensation—were just outward expressions of a deeper separation.

Try to feel what they felt—the identity-shattering experience of being defined solely by your affliction rather than by your individual value and worth as a unique human being.

This isolation tended to make the terrible final stage of the disease even more horrific. I ask you to forgive me in advance for planting this image in your brain, but victims sometimes spent their final hours lying alone, abandoned, being slowly devoured by wild animals, birds, and rodents while still alive.

All of these future terrors and horrors were wrapped up in those lepers' pitiful plea of *"Jesus, Master, have mercy on us!"* All of which makes another of Jesus' recorded encounters with a leper all the more remarkable. Earlier in Luke chapter 5, we find these words:

And it happened when He was in a certain city, that behold, a man who was full of leprosy saw Jesus; and he fell on his face and implored Him, saying, "Lord, if You are willing, You can make me clean." (v. 12)

Note that this man wasn't in the early stages of the disease. Luke reveals that this man was visibly "full of leprosy." You now have a better understanding of what was at stake for this precious individual.

Also note the state of his faith. He was sure Jesus *could* heal him. He just wasn't sure Jesus *would* heal him. Isn't that precisely where most Christians stand today? Maybe you stand in that very tension as you read these words. Few Christians doubt Jesus' power, ability, and authority to heal. But few have any confidence that He *will* heal them!

Few Christians doubt Jesus' power, ability, and authority to heal. But few have any *confidence* that He will heal them!

Our merciful Jesus understood this man's doubt. How do we know that? We see it in the very next verse:

Then He put out His hand and touched him, saying, "I am willing; be cleansed." Immediately the leprosy left him. (v. 13)

This man heard the most extraordinary words he'd ever heard or ever would hear. *I. Am. Willing.* Followed by the authoritative command, *"be cleansed."* But something even more extraordinary happened just before those words were spoken.

He put out His hand and touched him...

He touched him! And that touch had preceded the healing command. Jesus didn't wait for the man to be cleansed before bending down to put His divine hand on the back of the trembling, prostrate man.

This is the mercy of our Savior on full display: bending low to meet us, not where we should be, but where we are. Face down in dirt. Clinging to nothing but hope. In desperate need of mercy.

He touched him! Those words put me in remembrance of a song written by Bill and Gloria Gaither back in the early 1960s. The chorus of that song declared:

He touched me. Oh, He touched me,
And oh, the joy that floods my soul!
Something happened, and now I know
He touched me, and made me whole.[3]

Now let's return to Jesus' encounter with the ten lepers.

Mercy! If any group of individuals ever needed mercy, it was these. We will soon examine Jesus' response to that cry. But first there is one more relevant thing about leprosy in the Bible you need to understand.

Throughout church history, among the hundreds of "types" and symbols in the Bible, leprosy has been seen as a picture of sin and its effects. Key passages in Leviticus and Numbers point to this connection. And the more you understand about both leprosy and sin, the more parallels you see. Here are just a few examples.

First, just as leprosy causes a loss of sensation, habitual, repetitive sin has a "numbing" effect on the human conscience. And just as the loss of feeling in leprosy results in injury, infection, and loss of limbs, so sin causes us to damage ourselves without knowing it. And if we stay in those practices for a long period, we'll eventually find ourselves losing pieces of ourselves.

Those who abandon themselves to sin feel progressively less "alive," so they seek more and more self-destructive experiences simply in order to feel *something*. Anything. When sin reaches its ultimate destination in your life, you lose your affection for God, for life, and for people you ought to love and cherish.

Which means that sin, like leprosy, isolates us. And that's precisely what the enemy of our souls hopes to do. Just as a pack of hungry hyenas will attempt to cut a young gazelle out from the herd in order to devour it, so are Satan and his hordes of demons delighted when a person allows sin to isolate them from the safety of family and Christian community.

So, here's a question. What do sinners need just as desperately as those ten lepers did? Mercy! You'll recall that Jesus once cited a parable in which a despised tax collector beat his breast in prayer and cried out, "God be *merciful* to me, a sinner!"

We're all sinners and thus we're all in desperate need of mercy. And at times we're in desperate need of *healing* mercy. Here's wonderful news: Jesus is no less able to heal today than He was when He walked the earth twenty centuries ago. Nor is He any less willing.

In their darkest moment, something stirred within those ten lepers—a flickering flame of hope in desperation. Maybe they'd heard stories of this man Jesus who worked wonders of healing and restoration and deliverance—even among outcasts like tax-gatherers and fallen women.

Whatever sparked their courage, it led them to the audacious step of approaching Him. May I suggest to you that it is never a bad idea to approach Jesus when you're in need?

And then there are those six transformative words: *"Jesus, Master, have mercy on us!"*

Notice Jesus' response. Unlike His approach with the leper in chapter 5, He did not touch them and speak the blessing-command, *"Be cleansed."* Instead, He invited them into an act of faith: *"Go, show yourselves to the priests"* (v. 14), He said.

This instruction required them to step out in faith while still bearing all visible signs of their disease—to walk as if already whole before any evidence of wholeness was visible. In that space between the prayer and its answer lay a beautiful act of trust and obedience.

The story reveals that *"as they went, they were cleansed"* (Luke 17:14). In other words, their healing manifested as they were making the journey toward the nearest priest. But this story doesn't end with their physical healing.

While nine continued forward, rushing joyfully to get back to the life they thought they'd lost forever, one man—a Samaritan—turned back. He, and he alone, fell at Jesus' feet in gratitude.

Jesus noticed this response, asking, *"Were there not ten cleansed? But where are the nine?"* (v. 17) Then He spoke words that revealed a deeper reality: *"Arise, go your way. Your faith has made you well"* (v. 19).

The Greek word translated "well" here is *sozo*, and it speaks of complete restoration—not just of body, but of soul and spirit. In other words, complete wholeness in every part of a person's existence. While all ten experienced physical healing, this grateful soul received something more profound: total wholeness. It's good to get healed. It's far better to be "made whole."

Today, whatever burden you carry, whatever isolation you feel, whatever "uncleanness" you believe separates you from your heavenly Father, whatever is broken or out of order in your body—you're invited to voice your own short prayer.

Your Short Prayer:

Jesus, have mercy on me. I know You are both able and willing to make me whole!

CHAPTER 4

When You Desire Greater Influence for Jesus and His Kingdom

A 33-Word Prayer

And Jabez called on the God of Israel, saying, ***Oh that thou wouldest bless me indeed, and enlarge my coast, and that thine hand might be with me, and that thou wouldest keep me from evil, that it may not grieve me!*** *And God granted him that which he requested.*

(1 CHRONICLES 4:10, KJV)

"The Prayer of Jabez." More than twenty-five years ago, a best-selling book by that title took an obscure passage from the book of 1 Chronicles and made a short prayer world-famous. You will find that prayer in bold in the Scripture passage above.

Back in 2000 when that book first came out, the piece of that prayer that most people grabbed hold of was the "bless me" part. And there is nothing wrong with desiring God's blessing. Of course, a lot of Christians want to enjoy God's blessings without having to do the things that make them bless-able. Well, you're about to discover what made Jabez bless-able.

First, here is a little background to help you understand the context of this powerful little prayer. It explains why Jabez's life was never the same after God said "yes" to that little prayer. And as the Scripture verse above makes very clear, God did say, "Yes."

> *"And God granted him that which he requested."*

Names in the Bible are a big deal. So, we have to take note that the Hebrew meaning of the name "Jabez" is: "sorrowful" or "to grieve." Compare this to the fact that Jabez was from the tribe of Judah, which means "praise"! It's almost as if Jabez's name (identity) trapped him in a pattern that was contrary to his bigger, God-ordained destiny.

Living that way must have been hard, because Jabez's prayer is a cry for everything in his life to turn around.

He asked God to do four things for him:

1. To bless him indeed;

2. To enlarge his coast (territory);

3. That God's hand would be with him;

4. And that the Lord would keep him from evil that he might not be grieved (experience pain).

Maybe Jabez's tribal identity is a key to understanding why *"God granted him that which he requested."* You see, praise unlocks the windows of Heaven.

Yes, around the edges, Jabez's short prayer was a prayer for blessing and deliverance from pain, but at the heart of it is a prayer for favor and greater influence. It's right there in that request for enlarged territory and for God to be "with him."

Coastlines and rivers were how people marked the boundaries of their land in Jabez's day. When Jabez asked God to enlarge his coast, he was asking for an increase in the amount of land under his control.

Today, when God expands your territory, He is giving you greater influence for Him and for His Kingdom. And when God is "with you," it means you have favor wherever you go. That's the message of Psalm 5:12:

> *For You, O Lord, will bless the righteous; with favor You will surround him as with a shield.*

God told Abraham, *"I will be with you"* (Genesis 26:3, NIV). He told Moses, *"I will be with you"* (Exodus 3:12, ESV). As the Israelites prepared to enter the land of promise, Moses encouraged the Israelites, saying, *"The Lord your God Himself crosses over before you"* (Deuteronomy 31:3). As Joshua prepared to lead Israel's armies into Canaan, He told him, *"I will be with you"* (Joshua 1:5, NASB).

Are you beginning to see the pattern? Throughout the Bible, whenever God wanted to communicate that He wanted to give someone victory, favor, promotion, and expanded influence so they could carry out His good plans and purposes, all He had to say was, "I will be with you."

That's what Jabez is asking for here. When he prayed, "Enlarge my territory, Lord. Let Your hand be with me!" he was asking for victory, favor, and influence.

It's okay to ask God to give you more influence and favor so you can carry out your God-given destiny. When it comes to playing the role you were uniquely created for when He knit you together in your mother's womb, having greater influence and favor is a very good thing. And it's the right thing to ask for!

That's why I've prayed this prayer or something similar nearly every day of my life over the last few decades. And I have watched in awe, wonder, and gratitude as God has granted that request. God has expanded the "coasts" of the church I pastor. He has expanded the scope and reach of our television ministry. And I've watched as the impact of our various outreaches have gone to the farthest reaches of the globe.

When God expands your territory, He is giving you greater influence for Him and for His Kingdom. And when God is "with you," it means *you have favor* wherever you go.

One thing I have discovered is when you try to make a difference and do the things God made you to do, amazing things happen, like doors opening up to help you!

Yes, the things that motivate your heart matter. First Chronicles 4:9 says, "*Now Jabez was more honorable than his brothers...*" That suggests that Jabez's motives in praying that prayer were honorable as well.

James 4:2–3, the passage where we find the words "*You do not have because you do not ask,*" also tells us, "*You ask and do not receive, because you ask amiss, that you may spend it on your pleasures."* Several other translations of that verse say, *"because you ask with wrong motives."*

But make no mistake, our heavenly Father loves to bless! God delights in healing, delivering, providing, and protecting. These things are at the heart of who He is.

It's why a short, powerful prayer from an honorable man touched the heart of God. I'm convinced it was because this man named "pain and sorrow" knew how to praise his God.

As a member of the tribe of Judah, he was born into a family of praisers. I believe it is no accident or coincidence that on several occasions in the Old Testament, when God's people were facing an enemy army, it was the people of the tribe of Judah whom the Lord chose to go out first and lead the armies into battle (Judges 20:18; 2 Chronicles 13:15).

Countless preachers and teachers have taken note of this and encouraged God's people to lead with praise whenever they are under attack. That's good, biblical advice.

The greatest secret I can share with you about how to move out of a season of pain and sorrow is to develop the habit of praising God when things get hard. I have praised my way out of some of the most painful and difficult situations you could imagine. No matter what kind of hurt you're going through, you can praise your way out of it.

This is the secret to serving Jesus. It's the key to overcoming pain and sorrow!

As Jabez of the tribe of Judah discovered, you cannot praise God and remain sorrowful. You cannot praise God and stay defeated. You cannot continually, habitually praise God and *not* come out of any set of painful circumstances. It simply can't be done.

You cannot praise God in the midst of hurts and hardships and *not* see them turned into victories and testimonies. I simply cannot separate the fact that Jabez was of the tribe of Judah from the Bible's declaration that God said "yes" to his amazing 33-word prayer.

Maybe you started out in life with some disadvantages and hardships. Be encouraged. So did Jabez! His very name spoke of pain and sorrow.

Maybe you feel trapped in an identity that doesn't fit the destiny you know is yours in Jesus. Be encouraged. So did Jabez! Maybe you feel trapped in destructive generational behaviors or patterns of defeat. Be encouraged, so did Jabez!

When your mother names you, "One who causes pain and sorrow," you've gotten off to a rough start in life. But that simply didn't matter to Jabez. No one would have considered him a candidate for bigger territory, more favor, and greater influence. Yet he asked God for it. And God granted it.

Let me say it again. God loves to bless. And the very first part of Jabez's short prayer was, *"Oh, that You would bless me indeed"* (1 Chronicals 4:10). Clearly, that didn't offend God. The Hebrew word translated "bless" there is *barak* (בָּרַךְ), a word that can also mean "to congratulate."

That's because you can't congratulate someone without speaking out loud. And a *barak* is always spoken. Thinking kind thoughts about someone isn't a blessing in the *barak* sense of the word. It's not a blessing unless it's spoken. And when the One who spoke the stars and planets into existence speaks a blessing over you, you can be very sure things fly into motion.

The word *barak* appears hundreds of times in the Old Testament. More often than not, it is used to describe a human praising God. It's right there in Psalm 34:1, where David declares, *"I will bless [barak] the* Lord *at all times; His praise shall continually be in my mouth."*

Again, this is referring to something spoken. David is basically saying, "I'm constantly going to congratulate God on being so awesome and good and mighty and wonderful!" And it is no coincidence that David mentions "praise" in the very same breath.

Yes, we are to "bless" the Lord, but it is amazing to notice that, somehow, Jabez got a revelation that God wanted to "bless" as well as be blessed. And that He would do so if asked. Jabez clearly knew that when God decrees a blessing, it is a done deal.

It is vital and powerful to bless the Lord with praise and worship. But it is just as vital to believe, in faith, that God wants to bless you!

Barak can also mean "to lift up" or to "boost" higher. When you, like Jabez, cry out, "Oh, that you would *barak* me, Lord!" you're saying, "Father, give me a boost! I've been in the valley long enough. I'm stuck in a pit. Give me a boost up and out!"

But Jabez didn't just ask to be blessed. He said, "Bless me, *indeed*!" That last word makes the request exceptional. Or in other words, "Bless me real good, Lord! Bless me like I've never been blessed before!"

Now let's explore another part of this amazing short prayer. The part where Jabez asked God to "enlarge my coast."

Here is how other translations render that phrase:

- enlarge my territory (NIV, NKJV)
- expand my territory (NLT)
- enlarge my border (ESV)
- extend my border (NASB)
- give me a lot of land (CEV)

Isn't that a powerful thing to get up and pray every day?

God enlarge my coast today.
Entrust more to me and give me grace to steward it well.
Give me a wider platform of influence so I can
extend Your love and power to more people.
Grant me the ability to have a bigger impact on the world
for You and Your cause.
Stretch me. Enlarge me. Grow me!

Get up every day and pray, "Father, I praise and thank You for all You've done in the past. I'm so grateful. Now enlarge my coast. Give me more, Lord! Don't give me more than I can handle, but grant me the ability to handle more! Make me bigger in my faith! Bigger in my walk with You. Bigger in my testimony." But this wasn't the only thing Jabez requested of the Lord.

The third thing Jabez asked for is so very significant. He prayed, *"that Your hand would be with me."*

This part of his prayer reveals something very important. Jabez was not a prodigal, asking for his inheritance so he could go blow it on pleasures of the flesh. No, Jabez was asking for God's favor *and* God's presence. He clearly understood that having blessings without also having the Bless-er, is empty and meaningless.

The Hebrew word translated "hand" there is *yad* (יָד), which means "open hand." He's saying, "Lord, cause Your open hand to be with me." He's asking for an ongoing, personal touch.

This, too, should be a short, powerful prayer we pray every day. "God, give me all that You have for me, and be *with me* as I receive Your blessings to love others and glorify You."

So many people get material wealth or success and soon become so proud they think it's all their doing. They forget the God who blessed them with it. King Solomon is one example of someone who was blessed with wisdom and wealth, then squandered it on a thousand women who drew him away to their false, demonic gods instead of him leading them to his God.

Jabez wisely understood that no amount of success or blessing is worth anything without the greatest blessing of all—the presence of God.

Fourthly and finally, Jabez prayed, *"that thou wouldest keep me from evil, so that it may not grieve me!"* (KJV).

Remember, Jabez's name meant "sorrow" or "pain." In this part of his prayer, he's saying, "I don't want to be a victim of my name. I don't want my name to be my identity. I don't want to be trapped in my past."

No amount of success or blessing is worth anything without the greatest blessing of all—the *presence* of God.

In this final phrase of this amazing short prayer, Jabez seems to be saying, "I don't want to lose sight of who You are, God. And when You deliver me out of this valley of sorrow and pain, I don't want to forget that it is You who delivered me. You who boosted me up. You who enlarged my territory."

He's saying, "While I am being blessed, protect me from the temptation to forget You, so that I don't grieve You or me!"

Here is the wonderful news embedded in this 33-word prayer:

God wants to bless you. God wants a close relationship with you. God wants to give you all you can handle while He trains you to handle more. God wants to use you to bless your family, your community, and the nations.

Your Short Prayer:

Father, I thank and praise You for all You have done for me in the past. Now bless me in an even bigger way. Enlarge my capacity. Extend the borders of my influence and impact for Your Kingdom. Keep Your open hand of mercy, grace, favor, and power with me. May I never walk away from You in pride or ingratitude. May I never cause You, myself, or others sorrow or grief.

CHAPTER 5

When You Feel Like You're Going Under

A 3-Word Prayer

Then Peter got down out of the boat, walked on the water and came toward Jesus. But when he saw the wind, he was afraid and, beginning to sink, cried out, ***"Lord, save me!"***
(MATTHEW 14:29–30, NIV)

If you've gotten this far into this book, you surely know that powerful prayers don't have to be long ones. You don't need to use eloquent or big words to get help from Heaven.

In fact, the most powerful prayers are often the simplest and born of the deepest cry of our hearts.

This is so important to know because there comes a moment in every believer's journey when the waters of trouble rise so high, the winds howl so fiercely, and the night grows so dark that all human strength fails.

In that moment of utter desperation, a powerful prayer can and should rise up from the depths of your soul:

"Lord, save me!"

The most powerful prayers are often the simplest and born of the deepest cry of our *hearts*.

As we saw, that was Peter's cry in the key Scripture passage above. Now, please take note of the very next verse in Matthew's account:

> *And immediately Jesus stretched out His hand and caught him, and said to him, "O you of little faith, why did you doubt?"* (v. 31, emphasis added)

Aren't you grateful to see that word "immediately" situated right there at the beginning of that verse? When Peter cried out these words while sinking beneath the violent waves, the Savior did what only the Savior could do— He SAVED him! And He did so "immediately."

Lord. Save. Me. When our eyes are fixed on Jesus, these three one-syllable words carry supernatural power to part seas, calm storms, and summon the rescuing, redeeming, restoring hand of God into our desperate circumstances.

Of course, the key is keeping our focus fixed solidly on Jesus. It was only when Peter shifted his focus to his circumstances that he began to be overwhelmed by them.

Let's take a step back and learn about the amazing thing that happened right before this short, three-word prayer.

In the middle of the fourteenth chapter of Matthew, Jesus feeds the 5,000 men plus women and children with a young boy's sack lunch. Afterward, the disciples took up twelve large baskets filled with leftovers. In other words, they'd just witnessed a remarkable miracle of provision.

Next, Matthew 14:22–23 says:

> *Immediately Jesus made His disciples get into the boat and go before Him to the other side, while He sent the multitudes away. And when He had sent the multitudes away, He went up on the mountain by Himself to pray. Now when evening came, He was alone there.*

Do you see it? Jesus "made" His disciples head out onto the sea with a storm approaching. They weren't running *from* God's will—they were running straight into it!

And you know what happened next:

> *But the boat was now in the middle of the sea, tossed by the waves, for the wind was contrary.* (v. 24)

When you find yourself in trouble or facing opposition, do you sometimes think, *I must have done something wrong.* Or, *I must have missed God's will.* No, trouble comes through many paths and is simply a part of living in the fallen, broken world. And it's often totally unrelated to our mistakes or choices.

How many times have you questioned your worthiness to receive heavenly help when troubles arose? How often have you cried out, "What did I do wrong?" when the waves crashed around you? Hear this liberating word right now:

- Most times your storm is not punishment but preparation!
- Most times your trouble is not a sign of God's absence but evidence of His strategic positioning!

Here's great news. The very waters threatening to drown you today are the same waters God wants to use to display His glory!

Between the divine command to "Go" and your triumphant arrival on the other shore—your destiny—there often lies a storm that will test everything you believe. The disciples received the command to cross over, but before their destination came devastation. Before their arrival came anxiety. Before their victory came violent opposition!

Yes, at times you'll find yourself in troubled waters because you did what was right rather than what was popular, easy, or selfish. And, in that moment, you will be tempted to give in to panic or fear rather than trusting the Word you heard from the Lord. The disciples certainly experienced that temptation.

Remember, they had just seen an astonishing demonstration of God's power. Yet they seem to have forgotten it completely when fear came knocking. After all, Jesus had told them He'd meet them on the other shore!

Understand this: When God doesn't prevent your problem, look for Him to show up in the middle of it. That's exactly what the disciples experienced. In the midst of the storm, Jesus came toward them, walking on the water.

When God doesn't prevent your problem, look for Him to *show up* in the middle of it.

Trouble doesn't mean God has abandoned you. The disciples learned that Jesus may be out of sight, but He's never out of touch. To *"walk by faith, not by sight"* (2 Corinthians 5:7) means you'll sometimes walk in darkness without visible cues.

Take note of this: When the disciples' boat was being tossed like a cork on the waves, Jesus was up on a mountain praying for them! He was aware of the problem, and He was working on the solution. He was their mediator and their need-meeter.

The same is true for you. As Jesus sits at the right hand of the Father, He has one hand on your need and the other on your answer. Hebrews 7:25 declares that Jesus *"is also able to save to the uttermost those who come to God through Him, since He* ***always lives to make intercession for them****"* (Hebrews 7:25, emphasis added).

Can you imagine Jesus praying to the Father for His fear-filled disciples? And can you imagine the Father refusing to answer His prayers? Never! As Paul wrote, *"The Spirit Himself makes intercession for us with groanings which cannot be uttered"* (Romans 8:26). With both the Son and the Spirit talking to the Father on your behalf, your victory is guaranteed.

What's your crisis today? Is it a financial storm that threatens to sink your household? Is it mental or emotional oppression threatening to pull you under? Is it illness, rejection, loneliness, or guilt that, over and over, crashes against your soul like ocean waves?

When faith falls low and fear rises high, it's tempting to cry, "If only I had... !" or "If only I hadn't... !" We fall into the "woulda, coulda, shoulda" trap. But hear this prophetic declaration to you today: "It is not over until God says it's over." And He hasn't spoken defeat over you!

Your Bible proclaims that when night had fallen and all hope seemed lost, *"in the fourth watch of the night Jesus went to them, walking on the sea"*

(Matthew 14:25). The very element that threatened to destroy them became the platform for their deliverance!

But how did they respond to this miraculous visitation? Did they rejoice? No! Their fear was so intense, they cried out, *"It is a ghost!"* (v. 26). This is where believers need to be careful. Your fear has the power to distort your perceptions so dramatically that you can mistake your *answer* for another *attack*! What you think is a threat may actually be your deliverance!

I've seen a powerful truth at work time and again in my own life. When God removes the lesser, it is always to give you the greater! But you must have eyes of faith to recognize the Deliverer when He comes walking on the very waters you fear!

This brings us to two powerful, short prayers. In the middle of all that chaos, Peter prayed one of the boldest, most audacious prayers recorded in Scripture. He shouted a fourteen-word prayer: *"Lord, if it is You, command me to come to You on the water."* (Matthew 14:28) And Jesus replied with a one-word answer—*"Come."*

Jesus invited Peter to do the impossible. By the way, He's still extending the same invitation to His followers today. He invites us into a lifestyle of miracles in which we live out the truth that *"nothing will be impossible with God"* (Luke 1:37, ESV).

For a glorious moment, Peter walked where human feet were never meant to tread! The laws of nature bowed to the law of faith! Gravity surrendered to grace! The impossible became possible because one man dared to step out of the boat of comfort and security!

The laws of nature bowed to the law of faith! Gravity *surrendered to grace!*

But then the impulsive disciple's focus shifted from the face of his Lord to the ferocity of his circumstances. The howling wind, the crashing waves, and the physical impossibility of what he was doing all combined to distract and intimidate him. And Peter began to sink.

When Peter was scared and sinking, he didn't have time for fancy religious words.

He had no opportunity for religious formality. All he could utter was one of the most powerful prayers in Scripture: *"Lord, save me!"*

No prayer in history has ever been more effective or received a swifter response! Let me repeat what I pointed out previously. Scripture declares that *"immediately Jesus stretched out His hand and caught him"* (v. 31). Not tomorrow. Not after a committee meeting in Heaven. Not after Peter learned his lesson. Immediately!

This three-word prayer unleashed the supernatural power of God because it contained three essential elements:

1. **"Lord"—Recognition of Jesus' Lordship**
   Peter acknowledged Christ's supreme authority even in his moment of failure.

2. **"Save"— Admission of Our Helplessness**
   Peter confessed he had no power to save himself from his circumstances.

3. **"Me"—Personal Desperation**
   Peter made it intensely personal, crying out for individual rescue.

Your storm is not meant to drown you—it's meant to be the stage upon which God displays His power! The boat you're in may be taking on water, but it's surrounded by the presence of the water-walking Savior!

When human wisdom fails, when natural strength collapses, when your best efforts leave you sinking—that's when the three-word prayer becomes your lifeline to divine intervention: *"Lord, save me!"*

Take hold of the eternal, immutable promise of Romans 10:13 in faith and expectancy:

> *For "whoever calls on the name of the* L*ORD* *shall be saved."*

We worship a God who specializes in responding to desperate prayers with displays of power, signs, and wonders. They may seem puny, but your three words—"Lord, save me!"—can still move Heaven and earth today.

After Jesus rescued Peter and they climbed into the boat, the Word tells us the wind ceased. Then...

> *Then those who were in the boat came and worshiped Him, saying, "Truly You are the Son of God."* (Matthew 14:33)

When you cry out "Lord, save me!" in genuine desperation, He doesn't just change your circumstances—He changes your worship! He transforms your perspective! He elevates your faith!

That's why it's so important to understand that no storm lasts forever. It's a season, not a sentence. And after the rescue comes the revelation! After the saving comes the surrender! After the deliverance comes the declaration that Jesus is truly the Son of God!

No matter what impossible situation you face today—financial crisis, terminal illness, broken relationship, addiction, or depression—the God who commanded the laws of nature to bend for Peter is still in the business of supernatural intervention!

The God who commanded the laws of nature to bend for Peter is still in the business of *supernatural intervention!*

Redirect your focus from your circumstances to your Savior. Dare to cry out those three words with a heart of faith, trust, and expectancy. Then watch as the hand of divine rescue reaches down to lift you above the very waters that threatened to drown you!

Your Short Prayer:

Jesus, Son of God, Great King,

lover of my soul, Lord... save me!

CHAPTER 6

When You Need Deliverance from Trouble

A 130-Word Prayer

And Hezekiah received the letter from the hand of the messengers, and read it; and Hezekiah went up to the house of the LORD, and spread it before the LORD. Then Hezekiah prayed to the LORD, saying: ***"O LORD of hosts, God of Israel, the One who dwells between the cherubim, You are God, You alone, of all the kingdoms of the earth. You have made heaven and earth. Incline Your ear, O LORD, and hear; open Your eyes, O LORD, and see; and hear all the words of Sennacherib, which he has sent to reproach the living God. Truly, LORD, the kings of Assyria have laid waste all the nations and their lands, and have cast their gods into the fire; for they were not gods, but the work of men's hands—wood and stone. Therefore they destroyed them. Now therefore, O LORD our God, save us from his hand,*** *that all the kingdoms of the earth may know that You are the Lord, You alone."*

(ISAIAH 37:14–20)

Have you ever taken a letter with you to your prayer closet?

Maybe it was a huge bill you couldn't pay. Perhaps it was a medical report carrying bad news. It could have been from an attorney threatening legal action. Or even from someone you love—carrying words of anger, rejection, accusation, or hurt.

If so, you can relate to what King Hezekiah was doing in that passage from Isaiah.

Hezekiah—the righteous king of Judah—was showing God the letter he'd just received and was essentially waving it at Him saying, "Lord, open Your eyes. Take a good look at what the enemy is saying about You and Your people! Are you really going to let him get away with that?"

The "him" in that previous sentence is Sennacherib, the King of Assyria. And Assyria was one of the most powerful empires on the earth at that time. In fact, earlier in Hezekiah's reign he'd watched as Sennacherib's father, Sargon II, swept into Judah's northern neighbor, Israel, crushed all resistance, and carried ten tribes of Israelites off into captivity. So, he'd had a front-row seat for what an invading Assyrian army can do. And it wasn't pretty.

When you read all of Isaiah 36 and 37, you learn that Sennacherib had marched a massive army up to the borders of Judah. That army contained horses, chariots, and more battle-hardened soldiers than could be counted. And then King Hezekiah received that threatening letter from Sennacherib.

That letter not only threatened Judah with destruction if Hezekiah didn't bow down to him, but it also taunted and belittled Hezekiah's God!

Judah's little army was no match for mighty Assyria. So, Hezekiah took to his prayer closet and laid that letter out before the Lord.

In the process he prayed the relatively short prayer found in Isaiah 37. The key request in that 130-word prayer is found in these 11 words: *"Now therefore, O Lord our God, save us from his hand."*

Those words, born from "impossible" circumstances that threatened to destroy an entire nation, became the catalyst for one of history's most dramatic divine deliverances. King Hezekiah's prayer wasn't eloquent or lengthy—it was simply a desperate cry from a leader who knew exactly where to take his problem.

Sometimes the most powerful prayers are the ones that cut straight through our circumstances to the heart of God's character and authority.

Hezekiah's prayer teaches us that when we're facing our own impossible situations—when the medical report is devastating, when the financial crisis seems insurmountable, when relationships are crumbling—we don't need perfect theology or beautiful language. We need to know how to get our crisis to the right address.

We don't need perfect theology or beautiful language. We *need to know* how to get our crisis to the right address.

Picture yourself as King Hezekiah, ruler of the small kingdom of Judah, when a messenger arrives at your palace gates bearing an official letter. The seal belongs to Sennacherib, king of Assyria—a name that strikes terror into the hearts of every ruler in the ancient world.

Sennacherib wasn't just another neighboring king with a minor territorial dispute. Again, this was a conqueror who had systematically destroyed every nation that stood in his path—including Israel. The Babylonians had fallen. The mighty Egyptians had been pushed back. Kingdom after kingdom had been crushed under the chariot wheels of his state-of-the-art military machine.

Now, as King of Judah, you find yourself and your people right in the center of Sennacherib's crosshairs.

Sennacherib was more than just a skilled general. He was clearly also a master of psychological warfare. The letter Hezekiah received wasn't just a declaration of war; it was a carefully crafted instrument of intimidation designed to destroy confidence and breed fear.

The message was simple: "Don't be deceived into thinking your God will save you from me. I'm different from every enemy you've faced before. I have weapons and strategies you've never encountered. Your God may have rescued you in the past, but this time is different. This time, you're going to lose."

Does any of that sound familiar? The enemy of our souls uses the same tactics today. When a life crisis shows up on your doorstep, you're very likely to receive messages designed to intimidate you and cause you to collapse in fear.

Those messages arrive in the form of anxious thoughts that flood the mind in the middle of the night. They whisper in the echoes of the statistics the doctor quoted. (Or what "Dr. Google" told you when you made the mistake of looking up the diagnosis online.) The intimidating threats can shout through the foreclosure notice or the legal papers or the report from your child's school or from any of ten thousand other sources.

And the message is always the same: "This time is different. God may have helped you before, but this situation is beyond even Him."

Out in the world there's a saying describing someone in Hezekiah's situation: "He doesn't have a prayer."

But Hezekiah knew enough about the ways of God to realize that, in reality, *all* he had was a prayer. And when you have a God who is "more than enough," prayer is more than enough.

When you call on God in faith and expectancy, you're taking your cry for help to the "right address."

That's what I love about Hezekiah's response to that intimidating letter. He didn't ignore it, deny it, or try to handle it on his own. Instead, he did something that reveals great wisdom about how to deal with overwhelming circumstances.

Have you ever opened your mailbox and found a piece of mail meant for someone else? The Post Office does make mistakes occasionally. When that happens at our house, we usually write "Not at this address" on it and stick it back in the mailbox.

Or has one of the delivery companies ever left a package on your porch actually meant for one of your neighbors? Like most good people, you probably just walk it down the block where it belongs and leave it there.

Well, the Scripture tells us that when Hezekiah received and read the threatening letter, he immediately *"went up unto the house of the LORD, and spread it before the LORD"* (Isaiah 37:14). Think about that image for a moment. That's not a metaphor. Hezekiah literally took that piece of paper—with all its threats, intimidation, and psychological warfare—and physically laid it out in God's presence.

In other words, when the enemy sent Hezekiah that threatening letter, Hezekiah looked at the address and said, "This doesn't belong to me. This belongs to my God!" Then took it straight to where it belonged. He immediately redirected the crisis to the right address.

This is one of the most important principles you'll ever learn about prayer and faith. When the enemy sends you threatening "mail"—whether it's a medical diagnosis, a financial crisis, relationship problems, or any other form of bad news—your job isn't to carry that burden yourself. Your job is to get it to the right address as quickly as possible.

Most of us do the opposite. When bad news arrives, we tend to internalize it. We lie down with it, worry about it, let it torment our minds, and carry it around like a weight on our shoulders. But Hezekiah shows us a different way.

The moment you receive threatening news, get up! Don't lie down with bad reports. If you lie down with bad news, it will depress you, defeat you, and dominate your thoughts. Instead, immediately take that situation to your prayer closet—the place where you meet in intimacy with your heavenly Father—and lay it out before Him.

Notice how Hezekiah prayed when he spread that letter before the Lord. He didn't begin with his problems or his fears. He began by first establishing exactly who he was talking to:

> *"O Lord of hosts, God of Israel, the One who dwells between the cherubim, You are God..."* (v. 16)

Yes, Hezekiah started his prayer by reminding himself—and declaring to the enemy—exactly who his God is. *"Lord of hosts"* is a military term that literally means "Commander of the armies of Heaven." When you address God as the Lord of hosts, you're acknowledging that He commands supernatural forces you can't see but that are more real and more powerful than any earthly army.

Think about the armies God has at His disposal. He can use grasshoppers to defeat mighty warriors. He can employ hailstones as weapons. He can cause the minds of enemy generals to snap under pressure. He can confuse whole armies to such a degree that they attack and kill each other.

He commands forces of nature, circumstances, and armies of innumerable angels that can and will make the most sophisticated human military machine look like schoolyard children playing with toy soldiers.

Hezekiah started with that self-reminder, but that wasn't the only message in the opening words of his prayer. He also declared God's universal sovereignty: *"... You are God, You alone, of all the kingdoms of the earth. You have made heaven and earth"* (v. 16).

This wasn't just theological posturing. This was spiritual warfare. Hezekiah was reminding himself that his God wasn't a local deity with limited jurisdiction. No! The same God who created everything that exists, who rules over every earthly kingdom, was the God he was appealing to for help.

Hezekiah started his prayer by *reminding* himself—and *declaring* to the enemy—exactly who his God is.

This was followed by the beautiful simplicity of his plea: *"Incline Your ear, O Lord, and hear; open Your eyes, O Lord, and see; and hear all the words of Sennacherib, which he has sent to reproach the living God"* (v. 17).

Basically, Hezekiah was saying, "God, I need You to read this letter. I need You to see what the enemy is saying about You and Your people. I'm not asking You to fix *my* problem—I'm asking You to deal with this challenge to Your reputation and authority and good plan for Your people."

In other words, Hezekiah didn't make it solely about himself. He made it about something bigger. Something higher. He made it about God's name and glory and plans.

There's a great lesson in this for you and me. A lesson about effective prayer in crisis situations. Hezekiah shifted the focus from his problem to God's glory. He essentially said, "Lord, this isn't really about me or *my* kingdom. This is about what the watching world will think about You and Your Kingdom."

This is a powerful, game-changing shift in perspective for when you're facing your own crisis situations in life.

Whenever an intimidating, threatening "letter" arrives from the enemy, just remember: Don't view it as a threat to destroy you. View it as a prime opportunity for God to display His power, faithfulness, and love in a way that will cause everyone watching to know that He is God. And that He is glorious.

Your financial crisis is an opportunity for God to demonstrate that He is Jehovah-Jireh, your provider. Your health challenge is a platform for Him to reveal that He is Jehovah-Rapha, your healer. Your relationship struggles give Him space to show that He is the God who restores and redeems what the enemy meant for destruction.

When you begin to see your crisis as an opportunity for a display of God's glory rather than just a personal problem, it changes how you pray. Instead of begging God to fix your situation so you can be "safe" again, you start asking Him to show His power and faithfulness through your situation so that others will believe.

In other words, make it about His Name rather than your comfort.

The end of Hezekiah's story is one of the most dramatic divine interventions recorded in Scripture. After Hezekiah spread that threatening letter before the Lord and prayed that simple but powerful prayer, God responded through the prophet Isaiah with a message of complete victory.

That very night, the angel of the Lord went through the Assyrian camp and killed 185,000 soldiers. When Sennacherib woke up in the morning, he was surrounded by corpses. The mighty king who had conquered nation after nation fled back to his homeland in terror and humiliation, where he was eventually murdered by his own sons in a pagan temple.

One prayer. One night. Complete victory.

Here's what I hope you take away from this chapter. This dramatic intervention wasn't just about Hezekiah's military situation. It was about establishing a pattern for how God responds when His people know how to get their crisis to the right address. A pattern you and I can follow today.

The same God who commanded Heaven's armies for Hezekiah is available to you today. He's not limited by time, space, or circumstances. The question isn't whether He can handle your situation—the question is whether you know where to take your "letter."

When that threatening diagnosis arrives, when the financial pressure mounts, when the message of relational rejection arrives—no matter how impossible the circumstances seem—remember Hezekiah's response. Don't lie down with the bad news. Get up immediately and take it to the Lord. And by the way, in Jesus, you have far better access to your heavenly Father than Hezekiah did.

Don't lie down with the bad news. Get up immediately and *take it to the Lord.*

Spread your situation before Him. Not just metaphorically, but practically. Write down what the enemy is threatening. List the fears, the statistics, the worst-case scenarios. Literally place that paper before God and say, "Lord, this letter was sent to the wrong address. This belongs to You, not me."

Then shift into a mode of rest, confidence, and praise. Praise Him in advance of the defeat of your enemy. And then praise Him some more after it.

Your Short Prayer:

Lord of hosts, I spread this situation before You. Open Your eyes and see what the enemy is threatening. This crisis belongs to You, not me. Show Your power and faithfulness through this impossible situation so that everyone watching will know that You are God!

CHAPTER 7

When You Need a Refuge of Peace, Protection, and Provision in a Hostile World

A 14-Word Prayer

He who dwells in the secret place of the Most High shall abide under the shadow of the Almighty. I will say of the Lord, ***"He is my refuge and my fortress; my God, in Him I will trust."***
(PSALM 91:1–2)

When bombs are raining down upon your neighborhood, a refuge is a very important thing to have.

During the height of the Nazi Blitz of London in 1940, two teenage girls named Joan and Mabel were running for their lives through the pitch-black streets of London. Air-raid sirens screamed in the darkness as German bombers flew overhead, dropping their deadly cargo on the city below.

When a Luftwaffe plane roared directly over them and dropped a bomb on a nearby house, the terrified girls began crying and screaming for help. A woman heard their distress and emerged from the little homemade shelter she had crafted in her basement, offering them safety for the night. "Girls, do you want to stay in our shelter?" she asked kindly. "We have a bit of room."

Mabel wanted to accept, but Joan felt uneasy about it and insisted they make their way to her home where her father had constructed a strong, reinforced bomb shelter under their home. After some discussion, they thanked the woman and continued running through the dangerous streets until they reached Joan's house.

The next morning, Joan went out to survey the bomb damage—and discovered something that left her shaken. The very house where the kind woman had offered them refuge had taken a direct hit during the night. The woman and her entire family had perished.

In that moment, Joan realized that what seemed like the safest place on earth had become a tomb, while her decision to press on toward the refuge her father had provided for them had saved both girls' lives.

In a world filled with terrorism, disease, economic uncertainty, and spiritual darkness, we need to know that, for the child of God, there's a place of absolute safety, supernatural provision, and unshakeable peace.

As the opening verses of the 91st psalm tell us, that place is found *"under the shadow of the Almighty,"* and the key to accessing that place is found in what we *"say of the LORD."* Because what we say of the Lord opens doors for God to do what He longs to do in our lives.

If you're facing attacks that seem overwhelming, circumstances that appear hopeless, or fears that rob you of all peace and comfort—this ancient declaration and the verses that follow hold the secret to supernatural protection and provision that no natural or demonic spiritual power can touch.

The promise begins with a profound truth: *"He who dwells in the secret place of the Most High shall abide under the shadow of the Almighty"* (v. 1).

Notice that this protection isn't for occasional visitors or Sunday-only Christians. It's for *dwellers*—people who make their *home* in God's presence. The Hebrew word translated "dwell" here means "to remain, to settle, to make your permanent residence."

This isn't about a quick visit when you need something from God. Some Christians treat the God of the Universe like He has a drive-through window in His throne room in Heaven. No, this is about establishing your life in His presence, making time with Him your priority, and building your days around His Word and His ways.

Think about the difference between a hotel guest and a homeowner. A hotel guest passes through, stays temporarily, and has no real investment in the property. But a home-dweller lives there, maintains the property, knows every room intimately, and has all the rights and privileges that come with being a member of the household.

God is looking for dwellers, not visitors. He's looking for people who will make His presence their permanent address, who will build their lives around His Word, and who will prioritize relationship with Him above everything else.

God is looking for *dwellers*, not visitors. He's looking for people who will make His presence their permanent address.

Dwelling isn't just about church attendance, though that's important. It's not just about reading your Bible, though that's essential. It's about cultivating a lifestyle of abiding in God's presence—where prayer becomes as natural as breathing, where His Word becomes your daily bread, and where His peace becomes your default setting.

When you learn to dwell in the secret place, something amazing happens: you come under the shadow of the Almighty. Just like a little bear cub walking through the forest under the shadow of his massive father—the other animals don't fear the cub; they fear the giant standing over him. When you're under God's shadow, the enemy doesn't fear *you*—he fears the One whose shadow covers you.

In my many decades of walking with Jesus, I've discovered there are four essential keys to living daily *"under the shadow of the Almighty."* Yes, the 91st psalm holds four essential keys for living under divine protection and provision.

Key #1: Know Where to Dwell

As we've seen, the very first words of this psalm declare: *"He who dwells in the secret place of the Most High..."* This tells us that the first key is firmly making up your mind that God's presence is your primary residence. And how do you do that? You do it by:

- Making church a priority. Church isn't just a good suggestion—it's where you come to get your thinking right, where you come in mad and leave glad, where you come in feeling down but walk out lifted up. If you come to church and feel worse than when you arrived, something's wrong—either with the church or with your heart.

- Reading God's Word consistently. You can't dwell under the shadow of the Almighty if the only time you pick up the Bible is when you desperately need a word from the

Lord. The Bible is both milk and meat—nourishment for every stage of spiritual growth. You don't have to understand everything to be strengthened by it. Just read it, and let it read you.

- Building relationship, not just attending services. The *dwelling* experience was never just about a Sunday hour. It's about ongoing communion with the living God that affects every moment of every day.

Key #2: Learn How to Walk in Authority

The thirteenth verse of this glorious psalm in the King James Version says: *"Thou shalt tread upon the lion and adder: the young lion and the dragon shalt thou trample under feet."* This shows us that the second key is understanding that dwelling in God's presence gives you authority over every attack of the enemy. Notice there are three different deadly animals mentioned here.

The lion represents *expected* attacks. First Peter 5:8 calls the enemy of your soul a *"roaring lion."* When a roaring lion is after you, you know the attack is coming. The full verse in 1 Peter says, *"Be sober, be vigilant; because your adversary the devil walks about like a roaring lion, seeking whom he may devour."* Why should we be surprised when attacks come? Do we think the devil was going to send us a congratulations card when we got saved?

No—when you became God's child, you became Satan's enemy and, if able, he will attack you to hurt the heart of God. Notice that Peter said he is seeking those whom he *"may"* devour. These "lion-type" attacks should not be unexpected. And we have this divine promise that the Secret Place dweller will tread on the lion.

The adder (a venomous snake) represents *unexpected* attacks. These are the situations that come out of nowhere—the phone call that changes everything, the diagnosis that shocks you, the crisis that blindsides you. But even unexpected attacks will be overcome when you dwell in the Secret Place of the Most High.

The "dragon" represents *unfounded* attacks—worries and fears over things that aren't even real. Satan is a master at using worry as a weapon, painting pictures of catastrophe and convincing us that everything is going downhill. But dragons don't exist, and neither do most of the things we worry about.

Dragons don't exist, and neither do most of the things we *worry* about.

When you dwell in the secret place, God gives you power to tread over all three: the expected attack, the unexpected attack, and the unfounded attack. You put them under your feet through the authority of Jesus' name.

Key #3: Learn What to Say

In verse two the inspired psalmist declares: *"I will say of the Lord, 'He is my refuge and my fortress; my God, in Him I will trust.'"* This is the heart of the psalm and the key to supernatural protection: learning what to *"say"* about your God.

Let me ask you: What comes out of your mouth when trials come? What do you confess when circumstances look impossible? What do you speak over your family, your finances, your future, your health?

Again, the psalmist gives us a powerful principle when he writes: *"I will say of the Lord..."* This isn't just positive thinking. This is spiritual warfare.

What you say about God determines what God does in your situation. God talk brings God on the scene. Devil talk brings the devil on the scene.

Instead of talking to God about how big your problems are, talk to your problems about how big your God is. Instead of confessing defeat, confess victory. Instead of speaking death and disaster, speak life and blessing.

Joshua 1:8 echoes this secret of success: *"This Book of the Law shall not depart from your mouth, but you shall meditate in it day and night, that you may observe to do according to all that is written in it. For then you will make your way prosperous, and then you will have good success."*

Notice that God's Word must not depart from your mouth. Successful people—in business, in ministry, in life—learn to speak God's promises over their situations. They get up every day and declare: "This is the day the Lord has made. The favor of God is on my life today. I am blessed coming in and blessed going out. Whatever I put my hand to will prosper!"

Key #4: Set Your Love on Him

In the psalms, we usually hear the psalmist either talking *about* God or talking *to* God. But occasionally, we hear God Himself speaking. This is the case in the fourteenth verse of Psalm 91. There God declares: *"Because he has set his love upon Me, therefore I will deliver him; I will set him on high, because he has known My name."*

The *"he"* here is the person who has been dwelling under the shadow of the Almighty. Note the reason God promises to deliver such a person: *"Because he has set his love upon Me..."*

Do you see it? The final key is supreme devotion to God above everything else. This isn't just about paying lip service to the idea of loving God. No, it's about setting your highest and best love on Him. It means not loving the world more than you love Him. Not loving your family, your career, your possessions, or anything else more than you love Him.

When you set your affection on Christ, when you can honestly say, "I'd rather have Jesus than anything this world has to offer," something supernatural happens: God sets you on high. He elevates you above your circumstances, above your enemies, above every limitation that would try to hold you down.

Colossians 3:1–2 puts it this way: *"If then you were raised with Christ, seek those things which are above, where Christ is, sitting at the right hand of God. Set your mind on things above, not on things on the earth."*

This is what separates true dwellers in the presence of God from casual Christians. True dwellers refuse to go back to their old life. They don't spend Saturday night in the bars and Sunday morning in church. They don't live like the world six days a week and try to get spiritual for an hour or two on Sunday. When you really get saved, you don't want the old life—you want more of Jesus.

When you learn to dwell in the secret place, walk in authority, speak with faith, and set your highest, best love on Christ, God releases incredible promises over your life. Those promises include:

Divine Protection

Take note of verse seven of this psalm. *"A thousand may fall at your side, and ten thousand at your right hand; but it shall not come near you."* This isn't just about physical protection—it's about supernatural immunity to the destructions that devastate others.

Over the years I've heard many testimonies of combat soldiers who proclaimed the protection promises of the 91st psalm over themselves daily and came through horrific battles unscathed.

And parents can apply these same promises to their children. My mother-in-law, Pat, tells a remarkable story of when her brother, Larry, was a combat soldier—Army Special Forces (Green Berets)—during the height of the Vietnam War.

Of course, like every Christian mother who has sent a son off to a war on the other side of the world, Larry's mother prayed for her son's safety fervently and constantly.

One night she was awakened from a deep sleep with a sense of urgency to pray for her son's safety. She woke the rest of the family to join her in prayer. As she prayed, the Spirit of God led her directly to these lines from Psalm 91, and she stood and delivered them with faith and confidence, with the rest of the family in full agreement:

> *Surely He shall deliver you from the snare of the fowler*
> *And from the perilous pestilence.*
> *He shall cover you with His feathers,*
> *And under His wings you shall take refuge;*
> *His truth shall be your shield and buckler.*
> *You shall not be afraid of the terror by night,*
> *Nor of the arrow that flies by day,*
> *Nor of the pestilence that walks in darkness,*
> *Nor of the destruction that lays waste at noonday.*
> *A thousand may fall at your side,*
> *And ten thousand at your right hand;*
> *But it shall not come near you.* (vv. 3–7)

At that very moment, more than 9,000 miles away, her son had climbed aboard a troop transport helicopter. But just as the vehicle was about to take off, someone ran up to it and waved for Larry to get off of it. Orders for a different assignment had just come in.

So, the chopper left without him. A few hours later every man aboard had been killed in a fierce battle with the enemy. It was only later, when Larry told of that narrow escape, that his mother realized that it was the very night she and the family had laid hold of those lines at the altar of prayer.

You can live *in* the world but not be *of* it. You can be surrounded by chaos but walk in peace. You can face the same storms as everyone else but have supernatural stability because you're anchored to the Rock that cannot be moved. Yet this type of protection isn't the only one promised by this psalm.

Angelic Assignment

Verse eleven declares, *"For He shall give His angels charge over you, to keep you in all your ways."* When you dwell under the shadow of the Almighty, God assigns angels to watch over you. These aren't cute, chubby cherubs—these are mighty warriors of Heaven who have been given a specific assignment: your protection and provision.

You'll find a New Testament echo of this glorious promise in the closing lines of Hebrews chapter 1. Referring to the heavenly angels, the verse asks:

> *Are they not all ministering spirits* ***sent forth to minister for those who will inherit salvation?*** (v. 14)

Long Life and Satisfaction

We find more good news in the sixteenth verse: *"With long life I will satisfy him, and show him My salvation."* You see, God doesn't just promise you life—He promises you *long* life and satisfaction. You get to determine how long is long enough. When you're satisfied, then you're ready to go home. But until then, dwellers in the Secret Place can expect years of blessing, health, and fruitfulness.

Deliverance and Honor

The promise to the Secret Place dweller in verse fifteen is: *"I will deliver him and honor him."* Whatever you're trapped in, whatever has you bound, whatever seems impossible to overcome—God promises deliverance. And not just deliverance, but honor. He'll turn your mess into your message, your test into your testimony, your trial into your triumph.

That's just scratching the surface of the wealth of divine promises to those who create a lifestyle of living in God's presence. Yes, attacks will come. As we've seen, God's friends are Satan's enemies. If you belong to God, then God's ancient enemy considers you an enemy, too.

That's why it's absolutely vital to know what to say when trouble comes knocking. When attacks come—and they will come—you need to know what to say. Here's your full-length, personalized biblical faith-confession based on the promises and truths of Psalm 91:

> I will say of the Lord: He is my refuge and my fortress, my God, in Him I will trust. I will not be afraid of the terror by night, nor of the arrow that flies by day, nor of the pestilence that walks in darkness, nor of the destruction that lays waste at noonday.
>
> A thousand may fall at my side, and ten thousand at my right hand, but it shall not come near me. I dwell in the secret place of the Most High, and I abide under the shadow of the Almighty.
>
> He has given His angels charge over me to keep me in all my ways. I will tread upon the lion and the adder; the young lion and the serpent I will trample underfoot.

> Because I have set my love upon God, He will deliver me. He will set me on high because I have known His name. When I call upon Him, He will answer me. He will be with me in trouble; He will deliver me and honor me. With long life He will satisfy me and show me His salvation.

No, this isn't technically a "short prayer." It's actually four of five great short prayers rolled up together. When you say these things, you're not just reciting Scripture. You're wielding the sword of the Spirit against every force of darkness that would try to steal your peace, kill your dreams, or destroy your future.

This is a declaration of who God is and who you are in Him. When you learn to say the right things about the Lord, you position yourself to receive His supernatural protection, provision, and peace, no matter what storms may rage around you.

Today, whatever battle you're facing, whatever fear is trying to grip your heart, whatever circumstance is threatening your peace—remember that you have a refuge that no power on earth or in the heavenlies can touch. You can dwell in the secret place of the Most High and abide under the shadow of the Almighty.

There you are safe, secure, and supernaturally supplied for every need.

You have a *refuge* that no power on earth or in the heavenlies can touch.

Your Short Prayer:

God, you are my refuge and my fortress. In You I will trust. I dwell in Your secret place and abide under Your shadow. I will not fear what man can do to me, for You are the Almighty God. I tread upon every attack of the enemy—expected, unexpected, and unfounded. With long life You will satisfy me, and You will show me Your salvation. I set my love on You above all else, and You set me on high.

CHAPTER 8

When You Need Direction in a Crisis

A 9-Word Prayer

So David inquired of the Lord*, saying,* ***"Shall I pursue this troop? Shall I overtake them?"*** *And He answered him, "Pursue, for you shall surely overtake them and without fail recover all."*

(1 SAMUEL 30:8)

For David, the future king of Israel and Judah, it had been a bad day. A catastrophically bad day. In fact, it was probably the worst day David had likely ever experienced. And few if any of the days that followed in his long, eventful life would equal the darkness and despair of *this* day.

That's saying something because by this point in his life, David had already experienced more than his share of rough times. As a mere boy, he'd become an instant celebrity in Israel after killing Goliath and handing King Saul a major victory over his nemesis, the Philistines. Initially, Saul was grateful and had brought David right into his own royal household, but before long the obvious divine favor on David's life had provoked Saul's deepest insecurities and edged him toward insanity.

Saul tried on multiple occasions to kill David. Those couldn't have been good days. Ultimately, David had to flee into the wilderness and spent years of his life running from Saul and his men—living the life of a fugitive. Those weren't good days either.

When we get to 1 Samuel, chapter 30—where we find David in a place called Ziklag—he had already been living that fugitive life for years. The man who long ago had been anointed by the prophet Samuel as God's choice for the next king of Israel was basically a renegade warlord, roaming in exile with his family and own personal militia. That militia was a group of fellow outcasts who had wives and children but were basically living on the run with David and his family.

Yes, to understand the power of David's nine-word prayer, you need to picture the scene at Ziklag. David was twenty-nine years old, anointed as the future king of Israel but not yet on the throne. His insane father-in-law, King Saul, had been hunting him with assassins, forcing David to live as a fugitive with an army of six hundred men who were, in the words of Scripture, *"in distress," "in debt,"* and *"discontented"* (1 Samuel 22:2).

Ziklag represented David's "in-between place"—not Bethlehem where his story began, and not Jerusalem where his destiny awaited, but that difficult middle ground where God was preparing him for greatness. For one year and four months, David and his men had made this Philistine city their home while they waited for God's timing.

On this particular day, David and his army were returning from what they thought would be a routine campaign of fighting and plundering God's enemies, the Philistines. They were in high spirits, excited to see their families after months away. But as they approached the ridge overlooking their city, they saw an ominous black cloud of smoke rising from where their tents should have been.

Ziklag represented David's "in-between place"—not Bethlehem where his story began, and not Jerusalem where *his destiny* awaited, but that difficult middle ground where God was *preparing him* for greatness.

When they reached Ziklag, they found everything burned to the ground. The Amalekites had attacked while they were away. Every wife, every child, every family member had been taken captive. Their homes were destroyed, their hard-won wealth stolen, their loved ones gone.

The Bible tells us that *"David and the people who were with him lifted up their voice and wept, until they had no more power to weep"* (v. 4). These weren't just any men—these were battle-hardened warriors, men who had faced death countless times, men who had become accustomed to bloodshed and tragedy. Yet on this day, these mighty men wept until they couldn't weep anymore.

But grief eventually turned to rage, and that rage found a target: David himself. The very men who had followed him faithfully for years now spoke of stoning him. Everyone was grieved for their wives, sons, and daughters; in their pain, they needed someone to blame.

This is where we find David when he prayed his nine-word prayer. He, too, had lost everything—his home, his family, his wealth, and now the loyalty of his own men. He was standing in the wreckage of his former life, facing a decision that could determine whether he lived or died.

Have you ever stood, as David did, in the smoldering ruins of your life, wondering if you should fight back or just give up?

Maybe it was after receiving devastating news about your health. Perhaps it was the moment you discovered a spouse's betrayal. Or when you walked into your office to find a pink slip on your desk. It could have been while standing in the wreckage after a natural disaster destroyed everything you'd worked for. Or gripping the phone after learning about a tragedy that changed your family forever.

If so, you understand exactly what David was experiencing when he prayed those nine desperate words: *"Shall I pursue this troop? Shall I overtake them?"* (v. 8).

This wasn't a casual question asked during a quiet moment of reflection. This was a man standing in the ashes of everything he'd built, facing the most devastating day of his life, with his own men ready to stone him for their pain and loss. Yet in that moment of complete devastation, David asked the question that would determine not just his immediate future, but the destiny of an entire nation.

Should he pursue the Amalekites? It seemed obvious, but nothing about this situation was simple. The enemy had a several-day head start. David didn't know which direction they had gone, how many of them there were, or whether his grieving, angry men would even follow him into battle once again. And if he chose wrong, precious time would be lost—time that could mean the difference between rescuing their families or never seeing them again.

In that moment of decision in a crisis, before David asked God for direction, he did something that reveals the heart of true leadership in impossible circumstances. The Scripture says:

But David encouraged himself in the Lord *his God.*
(1 Samuel 30:6, KJV)

That's right. Before David sought guidance, he first found strength. He didn't allow the devastation to drive him away from God—he allowed it to drive him *toward* the Father. This is a crucial distinction that many of us miss when we're facing our own Ziklag moments.

When tragedy strikes, our natural tendency is to rely on our own wisdom, to panic, to blame others, or to sink into despair. Many blame God out of the same impulse that caused David's men to blame him. But David shows us a different way. In his darkest hour, when everything seemed hopeless, he chose to encourage himself in the Lord.

That presents a key question. What does it mean to encourage yourself in the Lord? In my years of preaching, teaching, and walking with God through a number of "Ziklag" days, I think I have an answer to that question.

I believe "encouraging yourself in the Lord" requires narrowing your focus to God and God alone. I'm talking about getting what I heard one preacher call "God Tunnel Vision." You focus on how mighty He is, how powerful He is, how faithful He is, how He'll never leave you or forsake you, no matter what happens.

Focusing solely on God pulls your eyes off of your circumstances, no matter how desperate and dark they may seem.

David looked at his circumstances—the burned city, the missing families, *his* missing family, the angry men—and chose to look beyond them to the God who had been with him when he faced Goliath, who had delivered him from the paw of the lion and the bear, who had protected him from Saul's spears. He remembered who his God *is* before asking Him what He wanted him to *do*.

Only after David encouraged himself in the Lord did he pray that crucial nine-word prayer: *"Shall I pursue this troop? Shall I overtake them?"*

Notice several important things about David's prayer. First, it was specific and practical. He didn't ask for a general sense of peace or some vague guidance. He asked two direct questions that required clear answers:

Should I go after them or not?

Will I succeed if I do?

Second, David asked from a position of humility and dependence. Even though he was an experienced military commander who had won countless battles, he recognized that this situation required more than human wisdom. He needed supernatural insight that could only come from God.

Third, David expected a clear answer. He wasn't looking for mysterious signs or trying to interpret dreams. He was asking his heavenly Father for the kind of practical guidance that a loving parent gives to a child in crisis.

The beauty of David's approach is that it worked. God didn't leave him hanging or give him some cryptic response. The answer came clearly and immediately: *"Pursue, for you shall surely overtake them and without fail recover all"* (v. 8).

Notice how specific God's response was. He didn't just say "yes" or "go after them." He told David that he would overtake the enemy and that he would recover everything that had been taken. God gave David not just direction but also the encouragement he needed to act on that direction in faith and confidence.

God gave David not just *direction* but also the *encouragement* he needed to act on that direction in faith and confidence.

The result was one of the most dramatic victories in David's military career. When they found the Amalekites, the enemy was *"spread out over all the land, eating and drinking and dancing, because of all the great spoil which they had taken from the land of the Philistines and from the land of Judah"* (v. 16). The Amalekites were celebrating their victory, completely unaware that justice was about to arrive.

David attacked from twilight until the evening of the next day. The Scripture records that *"not a man of them escaped, except four hundred young men who rode on camels and fled"* (v. 17). And then comes the beautiful refrain:

> *So David recovered all that the Amalekites had carried away, and David rescued his two wives. And nothing of theirs was lacking, either small or great, sons or daughters, spoil or anything which they had taken from them; David recovered all.* (vv. 18–19)

Please note the last three words of verse nineteen. In fulfillment of God's promise: *"David recovered all."* But he did more than that. Take a look at the next verse:

> *Then David took all the flocks and herds they had driven before those other livestock, and said, "This is David's spoil."* (v. 20)

Not only did David and his men get back what had been stolen, they walked away with even more than they had to begin with. This is the way of the God we serve, especially when we are willing to respond to a crisis with trust, faith, and obedience to Him.

But here's what makes this story even more remarkable: this victory occurred just before King Saul died in battle, paving the way for David to become king of Israel. David's nine-word prayer and the obedience that followed didn't just solve his immediate crisis—it positioned him for his God-ordained destiny.

This teaches us something profound about seeking God's direction in our own devastating moments. When we take time to encourage ourselves in the Lord and then ask Him for specific guidance, we're not just dealing with immediate problems—we're positioning ourselves to walk in God's good plans and purposes for our futures.

David's experience at Ziklag provides us with a practical pattern for navigating our own worst days. Let me close by sharing several principles we can draw from his example.

First, it's okay to weep.

David and his mighty men wept until they had no strength left to weep. Many people think that having faith means being immune to feelings, that tears somehow represent a failure of faith. But the Bible doesn't teach that. There's a time to weep, and weeping may endure for a night, but joy comes in the morning (Psalm 30:5).

The key is to weep with faith, knowing that another season of joy is coming. Don't let grief turn into unbelief or self-pity. You can cry and still believe that God has a plan to restore what the enemy has taken.

Second, refuse to get bitter.

When tragedy strikes, human nature wants to blame someone. David's men wanted to blame him. In our pain, we often look for someone to hold responsible—other people, circumstances, even God Himself. But bitterness is a poison that will destroy you from the inside out. As one minister puts it, don't just curse it, rehearse it, and disperse it. Instead, reverse it through the power of forgiveness.

Third, encourage yourself in the Lord.

This is perhaps the most crucial step. When your circumstances are screaming one message, you choose to focus on God's character instead.

You remind yourself of His faithfulness, His power, His love, and His promises. You command your emotional state to align with God's truth rather than your temporary circumstances.

Command your emotional state to *align with God's truth* rather than your temporary circumstances.

Fourth, ask God specific questions and expect clear answers.

David didn't pray vague prayers or look for mysterious signs. He asked direct questions and received direct answers. God wants to give you clear direction for the decisions you're facing. Be specific in your requests and trust Him to respond clearly.

Fifth, be ready to act immediately—boldly and in faith—on the direction you receive.

David didn't second-guess God's answer or look for additional confirmation. When God said *"pursue,"* David organized his men and started moving. Often that initial step of obedience opens up the next step in God's good plan.

The same God who answered David's nine-word prayer is available to you today. Your Ziklag may look different from David's, but the principles remain the same. Whether you're facing a health crisis, financial devastation, relationship betrayal, or any other form of loss, you can approach God with the same confidence David demonstrated.

God isn't trying to hide His will from you—He wants to guide your steps even more than you want to know which direction to go. Sometimes that direction will lead to immediate, dramatic victory like David experienced. Sometimes it will lead to a longer journey of faith and perseverance. But, either way, when you seek God's direction from a heart that's encouraged in Him, you can be confident that you're walking in His perfect plan for your life.

Your Short Prayer:

Lord, I'm standing in my own Ziklag moment. Show me clearly: should I pursue this situation or let it go? I trust You to guide me, and I'm ready to obey whatever direction You give me.

CHAPTER 9

When You Need to Lay Hold of a Promise by Faith

A 15-Word Prayer

Then the angel said to her, "Do not be afraid, Mary, for you have found favor with God. And behold, you will conceive in your womb and bring forth a Son, and shall call His name JESUS. He will be great, and will be called the Son of the Highest; and the Lord God will give Him the throne of His father David. And He will reign over the house of Jacob forever, and of His kingdom there will be no end." Then Mary said to the angel, "How can this be, since I do not know a man?" And the angel answered and said to her, "The Holy Spirit will come upon you, and the power of the Highest will overshadow you; therefore, also, that Holy One who is to be born will be called the Son of God."... Then Mary said, ***"Behold the maidservant of the Lord! Let it be to me according to your word."***

(LUKE 1:30–35, 38)

Here is a helpful way to tell whether a vision, dream, or promise is really from God: It seems impossible. Of course, it would! He is the God of the impossible. Why would God go around giving His people visions and promises that can be realized through human effort? When it's a God dream or vision, you look at it and cry, "How could that ever happen?"

That's exactly what Mary, the mother of Jesus, does in the first chapter of Luke when the angel Gabriel appears to her with some of the most shocking news any human has ever received. And, in that passage, she gives us a beautiful "short prayer" example of how to respond to an impossible promise from God.

"Let it be to me according to your word."

These nine words, spoken by a teenage girl in a moment that would change the course of human history, represent one of the most powerful faith-filled short prayers ever recorded.

Young Mary—just a righteous teenage country girl from a small town in Galilee—didn't fully understand what was being asked of her. She couldn't see how it would be possible. But she also knew if that promise was true—and she clearly believed it was—the fulfillment of that promise would cost her her reputation, her security, and perhaps even her life. But when confronted with God's impossible promise, she made a choice that every believer must eventually make—the same choice God invites you to make in a grand adventure:

She took a leap of faith and surrendered to His Word.

If you've ever received a promise from God that seemed too big, too impossible, or too costly—Mary's response holds the key to seeing that promise fulfilled. Because when we learn to pray, "Let it be to me according to Your word," we position ourselves to receive miracles that defy human logic and divine interventions that change everything.

The story begins with a significant greeting. An angel appears to a young virgin and exclaims: *"Rejoice, highly favored one, the Lord is with you; blessed are you among women!"* (Luke 1:28).

When we learn to pray, "Let it be to me according to Your word," we position ourselves to receive *miracles* that defy human logic and *divine interventions* that change everything.

Notice the angel's first words: *"highly favored one."* Before Mary ever did anything to earn it, before she ever proved her worthiness, before she even understood what was being asked of her—she was already highly favored by God.

We tend to undervalue the power of favor these days. But favor from God is one of the most powerful things you can obtain. King David said, *"For You, O Lord, will bless the righteous; with favor You will surround him as with a shield"* (Psalm 5:12). The favor of God protects you. It goes before you, opening doors and preparing the way. Having the favor of God on your life is a wonderful thing.

Over the years I've discovered that this is where impossible promises begin: with the recognition that you have found favor with God. Not because you're perfect, not because you have everything figured out, not because you're more qualified than anyone else—but simply because God has chosen to set His love upon you.

Mary's response was very human: *"She was troubled at his saying, and considered what manner of greeting this was"* (Luke 1:29). *Me?* She must have thought as she looked over her shoulder to see if someone else had walked into the room. *You're talking to little me? The hillbilly girl that people over in*

Jerusalem would look down their noses at because of my country accent? It was a startling, even frightening thing to hear from the mouth of an archangel.

There is a good lesson in that for us. When God speaks impossible things over our lives, our first reaction is often confusion and fear. We wonder what this means, why us, and how it could possibly come to pass.

But the angel's next words just reinforce the message of favor so Mary cannot miss the message: *"Do not be afraid, Mary, for you have found favor with God"* (Luke 1:30).

Fear is the enemy of faith, so when God gives us impossible promises, He follows them with the reassurance that we don't need to be afraid. His favor is upon us, and that changes everything.

The angel then delivers one of the most impossible announcements in human history:

> *"And behold, you will conceive in your womb and bring forth a Son, and shall call His name* Jesus. *He will be great, and will be called the Son of the Highest; and the Lord God will give Him the throne of His father David. And He will reign over the house of Jacob forever, and of His kingdom there will be no end."*
> (Luke 1:31–33)

Mary's response was perfectly understandable: *"How can this be, since I do not know a man?"* (Luke 1:34). In other words, "I know how babies are made. How am I going to 'conceive' and 'bring forth a Son?'"

It's possible for us to have a similar response when God plants a vision in our hearts. When God whispers dreams into our spirits, when He tells us we're going to touch lives, build something significant, or make a difference in this world, our immediate response is often the same as Mary's: "How can this be? I don't know the right people. I'm not smart enough, talented enough, or connected enough."

Notice that Mary didn't say, "*Will* this really be?" She said, "*How* can it be?" There's a key difference. In other words, she wasn't expressing doubt in the truth of Gabriel's message. She was expressing curiosity about the process. And Gabriel was happy to answer that "how" question.

"The Holy Spirit will come upon you, and the power of the Highest will overshadow you" (Luke 1:35). In other words, "You qualify for the miracle fulfillment of this promise because you have *Me*. You don't need human connections, or credentials, or degrees when you have Holy Ghost power. You don't need natural ability when you have God on your side."

The angel's declaration contains one of the most powerful truths in all of Scripture. A truth that should be in the forefront of our minds and hearts every moment of every day:

"For with God nothing will be impossible" (Luke 1:37).

This wasn't just about Mary's situation—this is a universal principle that applies to every impossible promise God has ever given to any of His children. And that includes you.

The "how" question is where most people get stuck. We want to see the plan before we're willing to believe the promise. We want to see the path before we're willing to take the first step. We want to have all the answers before we're willing to say yes to God.

But here's what I've learned about God's promises: He rarely shows us the whole plan upfront. Why? Because if we could figure out how He was going to do it, we wouldn't need faith and, without faith, it's impossible to please God. We are called to walk by faith, not by sight (2 Corinthians 5:7).

God will show us what to do next. Usually, the first thing is to let go and trust Him.

To say "yes" to God. This is exactly what Mary did with her short prayer. Mary quickly arrived at the moment that changed everything:

> *Then Mary said, "Behold the maidservant of the Lord! Let it be to me according to your word."* (Luke 1:38)

This is the prayer that unlocks miracles. This is the moment when arguing stops and faith begins. This is where Mary stopped trying to figure it out and started trusting God to work it out.

God will show us what to do next. Usually, the first thing is to *let go and trust Him.*

"Let it be to me according to your word" is a prayer of complete surrender. The old-timers would call this a "prayer of consecration." It's an important kind of prayer for every believer. It's saying, "God, I'm Yours. If you say 'go,' I'll go. If you tell me to say it, I'll say it. I don't understand how this is going to work, but I believe what You've said. I don't see how it's possible, but I trust that You can do the impossible. I'm available for whatever You want to do in my life, even if it costs me everything. I'm a big YES for you."

All of that and more was contained in Mary's fifteen-word prayer. Notice what Mary *didn't* say. She didn't say, "Let me think about it and get back to You." She didn't say, "Let me pray about it." She didn't say, "Let me counsel with others first." No, she said, "Let it be to me according to your word"—right now, right here, without reservation, qualification, or delay.

This is the kind of trusting, faith-filled response that moves Heaven. When God finds someone who will stop arguing, stop questioning, stop demanding more information, and simply say, "According to Your word, Lord"—that's when miracles begin to unfold.

What I love about Mary's story is what she did after the angel left. She held on to her "yes." She stayed in trust and in faith. She didn't let the promise wear off when the hardness of reality set in and circumstances became difficult.

Here's what you need to understand: when God gives you a word, if you let it, it will wear off. The clarity, the enthusiasm, the fire, the passion you felt when God first spoke to you—the enemy will try to rub that out. Whatever God promised you, whatever He told you He wanted to do in your family or your life, it will start to evaporate like the morning dew if you don't guard it.

It's one thing to have faith when the angel is still there. It feels good when God's speaking to you in a worship atmosphere where His Spirit is moving freely. But then you walk out, get in your car, go home, and reality hits you in the face. Then comes that voice: "You got caught up in the moment. That was just your emotions. You better not listen to that voice inside."

But Mary held on. When people began to talk, when circumstances looked impossible, when her pregnancy began to show and the whispers started—she remembered what the angel said and held on to God's Word.

And notice what she declared even in the midst of difficulty:

> *"My soul magnifies the Lord, and my spirit has rejoiced in God my Savior. For He has regarded the lowly state of His maidservant; for behold, henceforth all generations will call me blessed."* (Luke 1:46–48)

Mary seems to have understood something profound. She may have said to herself: "Right now it looks like a bad deal. Right now I'm pregnant out of wedlock. Right now they're whispering about me and saying ugly things. Right now they think I've lost my mind. But the Word of the Lord that came through the angel said that a day is coming when they will call me *blessed*."

This is faith's perspective: the ability to see past present difficulties to future fulfillment. Mary could endure the temporary shame because she could see the eternal glory. She could handle the present misunderstanding because she knew about the coming promise. This is the difference between the fear of the Lord and the "fear of man."

Mary's story contains a pattern that runs throughout Scripture. A pattern captured in Jesus' declaration: *"Many are called, but few are chosen"* (Matthew 22:14, NASB). Many people receive words from God, but few are chosen to see those words fulfilled. Why? Because few are willing to pay the price of holding on when it gets difficult.

Being chosen isn't about having a special ability—it's about having a special heart. It's about being willing to stay faithful when others give up. To keep believing when circumstances seem to contradict the promise. To remain yielded and available when it would be easier to quit.

God allows you to do something extraordinary not to give you glory and honor, but so you can glorify Him. And the only way to do that is to remain broken before Him, to never forget where He brought you from, to constantly acknowledge that without Him, you can do nothing.

Every believer who walks out God's highest and best plans for their lives was chosen not because they're more talented, but because they've learned to say "Yes, Lord," and mean it.

Maybe as you're reading this, God has already spoken something impossible into your life. Maybe He's told you that you're going to impact your family, your community, your nation. Maybe He's given you dreams that seem too big, promises that appear impossible, a calling that feels overwhelming.

If so, you're in the same position Mary was in. You can argue with God about all the reasons it won't work, or you can surrender to His word and watch Him do the impossible.

Remember, you have found favor with God. Not because you're perfect, but because He has placed His covenant love upon you. You don't need all the right connections when you have the Holy Spirit. You don't need natural ability when you have supernatural power. You don't need to understand the "how" when you know the "who."

The same God who enabled a virgin to conceive the Savior of the world is the God who wants to do impossible things through your life. The question is: are you willing to stop arguing and start surrendering?

"Be it to me, Lord, according to your word!"

You don't need to understand the "how" when you *know* the "who."

This prayer contains everything you need to see God's impossible promises fulfilled in your life. It begins with surrender, continues with faith, and ends with availability. When you can honestly pray these words and mean them, you position yourself to receive miracles that will amaze you and bless generations to come.

The same power that overshadowed Mary is available to overshadow your impossibilities today. The same God who regarded the lowly estate of a teenage girl regards your situation with favor and love. And the same faithfulness that enabled Mary to carry the Savior of the world will enable you to carry whatever assignment God has given you.

Your Short Prayer:

Lord, I don't understand how You're going to do what You've promised, but I believe Your word. Let it be to me according to Your word. Whatever it is You've called me to do... the answer is "yes."

CHAPTER 10

When You Feel Broken or Like You're Falling Apart

A 9-Word Prayer

And he said unto Jesus, ***Lord, remember me when thou comest into thy kingdom****. And Jesus said unto him, Verily I say unto thee, Today shalt thou be with me in paradise.*

(LUKE 23:42–43, KJV)

"Lord, remember me when thou comest into thy kingdom." These nine words, gasped out in the final moments of a dying thief's life, became one of the most profound prayers ever recorded in Scripture. Spoken between ragged breaths on a cruel Roman cross, they carried the weight of a lifetime of regret, the desperation of impending death, and the flickering hope of redemption.

But here's what makes this prayer so remarkable: the thief wasn't asking Jesus to simply think about him or call him to mind. He was crying out for something far more powerful—something that could transform his broken, dismembered life into something whole and beautiful again.

To fully understand the depth of this simple prayer, we need to journey back to that dark hill called Calvary and see what was really happening in those final hours of Jesus' earthly ministry.

Picture yourself standing at the foot of Calvary, looking up at three figures hanging in agony against the darkening sky. In the center hangs Jesus of Nazareth, the man who claimed to be the Son of God. On either side hang two thieves—criminals who had lived lives of violence and lawlessness, now facing the brutal Roman method of execution reserved for the worst offenders.

But to truly understand what happened that day, we need to shift our perspective. Instead of looking up from the ground, imagine seeing the scene from Jesus' vantage point—hanging on that cross, looking down at the chaos below, and listening to the conversations happening around Him.

The Gospel writers Matthew and Mark both record that, initially, both thieves joined the crowd in mocking Jesus. They hurled insults and blasphemies at the man hanging between them, adding their voices to the chorus of ridicule rising from the religious leaders and soldiers below.

But something extraordinary happened to one of those thieves in his final moments. As death approached and eternal destiny became crystal clear, a transformation took place that would echo through eternity.

Nine words, prayed in desperate hope. Born of the recognition that he was in the presence of pure divinity in human form:

Lord, remember me when thou comest into thy kingdom.

At first glance, this might seem like a simple request for Jesus to think about him in the future. But the word "remember" in the ancient language of the Israelites carries a meaning far deeper than our modern understanding suggests.

In our day, to "remember" someone means to call them to mind, to think about them, to bring them into our mental awareness. But, in the ancient world, particularly in Hebrew thought, the word carried the deep meaning of restoration and reassembly. And although Luke is writing in Greek, he knows he is addressing readers who think in Hebrew.

There are hints of this even in English. To "dismember" something is to tear apart, to separate, to rip into pieces. When someone was dismembered, they were broken, divided, destroyed. To undo such damage would be to re-member. So to "remember" is to put back together what has been torn apart or separated. To restore what has been broken. To reassemble what has been scattered.

> **To "remember" is to put back together what has been torn apart or separated. To *restore* what has been broken.**

In the light of this understanding, we see that this dying thief wasn't simply asking Jesus to think about him occasionally when He got to Heaven. He was crying out from the depths of his broken soul: "Lord, I'm torn apart! I'm dismembered by sin, by shame, and by the consequences of my choices. When You come into Your Kingdom, put me back together! Restore what has been broken! Reassemble what has been shattered!"

What makes this prayer even more remarkable is what the thief recognized about Jesus, even in His apparent moment of defeat. Looking at a man crowned with thorns, covered in blood, and dying on a cross, this criminal saw royalty. Despite Jesus' physical condition, the thief addressed Him as "Lord" and spoke of His "Kingdom."

This reveals the supernatural insight that can come by grace to the human heart in moments of desperate need. While others saw only a denounced rabbi, this dying man recognized the King of Kings hanging beside him.

Jesus' response to this broken man's prayer was immediate and breathtaking:

> *Verily I say unto thee, Today shalt thou be with me in paradise.*
> (Luke 23:43, KJV)

Even as His lifeblood flowed from His body, grace flowed from His lips. This is our Savior. This is our Redeemer.

The word "paradise" that Jesus used is the same word often used to describe the garden of Eden—that perfect place where God originally walked with mankind in unbroken fellowship. It was the place from which Adam and Eve had been banished when sin entered the world, causing the first great "dismembering" of the human race from their Creator. The great, tragic "separation."

In essence, Jesus was saying to this thief: "You asked Me to remember you—to put you back together—when I come into my Kingdom. But I'm going to do something even better. Today—this very day—you're going back to paradise. You're going back to the garden. What was dismembered in Eden is going to be re-membered through Me and this cross."

Can you imagine the wonder that must have filled that dying man's heart? He had asked for future restoration, but Jesus promised immediate paradise. He had hoped for eventual remembrance, but Jesus offered instant reconciliation.

This beautiful exchange between Jesus and the thief reveals a pattern that runs throughout all of Scripture—the pattern of dismembering and remembering, of breaking apart and putting back together.

Think about what happened at the Tower of Babel. Humanity had come together with one language and one purpose, but their hearts had turned away from God toward idolatry. So God confounded their languages and scattered them across the earth (Genesis 11:1–9). The human race was dismembered, divided, separated.

But on the day of Pentecost, God began the great work of remembering—putting back together what had been scattered. When the Holy Spirit fell on the disciples, they began to speak in tongues that transcended all national and ethnic barriers (Acts 2:1–11). God was restoring what had been divided, re-membering what had been dismembered.

Consider what happened to Jesus Himself on the cross. His body was torn, causing the life-giving force of His blood to drain out of Him through the wounds in His hands, feet, and side. According to Leviticus 17:11, *"the life of the flesh is in the blood"* because when blood is separated from a body, that body dies.

But here's the beautiful mystery of Communion: when we take the bread representing His body and the cup representing His blood, we are participating in the great re-membering. We're putting back together what was separated. We're declaring that what death dismembered, faith remembers.

When we take the bread representing His body and the cup representing His blood, we are participating in the great *re-membering*.

It is no wonder that only hours earlier, at the Last Supper, Jesus had told His disciples, "*... do this in **remembrance** of me*" (Luke 22:19, NIV).

Every time we partake of Communion with genuine faith, we're not just remembering Jesus in the sense of thinking about Him. We're participating in the restoration He purchased with His life. We're declaring that broken lives can be made whole, that scattered pieces can be reassembled, that what sin has dismembered, grace can re-member.

Perhaps as you read these words, you're feeling the effects of dismemberment in your own life. Maybe sin has torn apart your relationships, your peace, or your sense of purpose. Maybe addiction has dismembered your will from your values. Maybe trauma has separated your heart from your ability to trust and love.

Or maybe it's your family that feels dismembered—children scattered by rebellion, marriages torn apart by betrayal, parents and children separated by misunderstanding and hurt.

Maybe it's your dreams that have been dismembered—broken by disappointment, shattered by circumstances beyond your control, torn apart by the harsh realities of life.

Whatever has been dismembered in your life, the same Jesus who heard that thief's plea on Calvary is ready to hear yours today. He specializes in putting back together what has been torn apart. He is the great Rememberer—the One who restores what has been broken and reassembles what has been scattered.

> **He specializes in putting back *together* what has been torn apart.**

What I love about the thief's prayer is how simple it is. He didn't have time for big speeches or elaborate religious rituals. He was dying, and he knew it. All he had was a simple recognition of who Jesus truly was and a fleeting opportunity to utter a desperate cry for restoration.

"Lord, remember me."

That's it. No complicated formulas. No perfect doctrine. No religious credentials. Just a broken man crying out to the only One who could put him back together.

And Jesus responded immediately. Not because the thief had lived a good life—he admitted he deserved his punishment. Not because he had followed all the religious rules—he was a criminal hanging on a cross. Jesus responded because, in that moment, the thief demonstrated the one thing that always moves the heart of God: simple, desperate faith.

This is the beauty of short prayers. They don't need perfect theology about God or fancy words. They require only honest hearts crying out to the God who specializes in restoration.

When Jesus promised the thief that he would be with Him "today" in paradise, He was offering something that goes far beyond our usual understanding of Heaven. Paradise isn't just a place we go when we die—it's the restoration of everything that was lost when sin entered the world.

Paradise is the place where the dismembered become re-membered. It's where broken relationships are restored, where shattered dreams are made whole, where scattered families are reunited, where wounded hearts are healed.

And here's the amazing thing: while the fullness of paradise awaits us in eternity, the process of remembering—of putting back together what has been torn apart—can begin today. Right now, in this moment, Jesus can begin the work of restoration in your life.

The same power that promised paradise to a dying thief is available to you today. The same grace that turned a criminal's final moments into a doorway to eternal life can transform your current circumstances into a testimony of God's restoring power.

In the early church, believers understood two very profound things about Communion that many of us have lost. They saw it first not just as a memorial meal but as a participation in the great work of remembering—becoming mindful of and grateful for—all that Jesus accomplished on the cross.

Secondly, as they took the bread and cup, they were declaring that what death had dismembered, faith was remembering. They were proclaiming that broken lives could be made whole, that scattered people could become one body, that what sin had torn apart, love could put back together.

This is why the apostle Paul warned that we should examine ourselves before partaking of Communion (1 Corinthians 11:28). Not because we need to be perfect, but because we need to come with the same heart as that dying thief—recognizing our need, acknowledging Jesus as Lord, and crying out for Him to remember us.

When you come to the table of the Lord, you're not just remembering what Jesus did two thousand years ago. You're participating in what He's doing *right now*—the ongoing work of putting back together what has been torn apart in this sin-ravaged world.

Maybe today you need to pray the same prayer as that dying thief. Maybe your life feels dismembered, torn apart by circumstances, sin, or heartbreak. Maybe you need the great Rememberer to put back together what has been scattered.

Your circumstances don't disqualify you from God's grace. Your past doesn't prevent you from experiencing His restoration. Your brokenness doesn't make you unworthy of His love.

The same Jesus who heard the cry of a dying criminal will hear your cry today. The same grace that transformed a thief into a saint can transform your life into a testimony of God's restoring power.

The thief asked to be remembered when Jesus came into His Kingdom. But Jesus promised him paradise that very day. When you cry out to God for restoration, don't be surprised if He does more than you ask or imagine. Don't be surprised if the remembering begins immediately.

When you cry out to God for *restoration*, don't be surprised if He does more than you ask or imagine.

The power of the following prayer isn't in its length or eloquence—it's in its honesty and faith. It's in the recognition that we need restoration and that Jesus is the only One who can provide it. When you pray this prayer with genuine faith, you're not just asking God to think about you. You're asking Him to put you back together, to restore what has been broken, to remember what has been dismembered.

And He will. Because that's what He does. He remembers. He restores. He puts back together what has been torn apart. That's the promise of the cross, the hope of the gospel, and the power of simple, desperate faith.

Your Short Prayer:

(Consider taking Communion as you pray this prayer.)

Lord, remember me. Put back together what has been torn apart in my life. Restore what has been broken. Replenish what has been lost. I know I don't deserve it, but I believe You are able and willing to make me whole. Remember me, Lord, and bring me into Your paradise of restoration, renewal, and revival.

CHAPTER 11

When a Loved One Needs a Miracle

A 7-Word Prayer

So Jesus came again to Cana of Galilee where He had made the water wine. And there was a certain nobleman whose son was sick at Capernaum. When he heard that Jesus had come out of Judea into Galilee, he went to Him and implored Him to come down and heal his son, for he was at the point of death.... The nobleman said to Him, ***"Sir, come down before my child dies!"***
(JOHN 4:46–49)

Can you feel the desperation in the seven simple words of this father's plea to Jesus? Read between the lines. Activate your God-given imagination. Hear the trembling urgency in that nobleman's voice:

"Sir, come down before my child dies!"

There is so much truth to be gleaned from this short passage from the pen of the disciple that Jesus loved. Truth about God's heart of compassion. Truth about Jesus' power to heal. Truth about the power of a short prayer.

Throughout this book I'm hoping to ignite your faith concerning the extraordinary power of short prayers. And this passage gives me a prime opportunity!

Some of us think we need to pray for hours to move the hand of God. Some believe our prayers must be eloquent, filled with Scripture and theological precision. But sometimes the most powerful prayers are the shortest ones!

When that nobleman ran to Jesus, he didn't bring a prepared sermon. He didn't quote the Torah. He didn't even say "please"! His heart was too broken for formalities. His son lay dying! All he could come up with was a desperate cry for Jesus to come.

Can I tell you something? He's not counting your words; He's weighing your faith. And here in the nobleman's encounter with Jesus, we find several key truths about healing specifically and miracles in general.

First, let's see how Jesus responded to this prayer and how the nobleman reacted to Jesus' response!

> *Jesus said to him, "Go your way; your son lives." So the man believed the word that Jesus spoke to him, and he went his way. And as he was now going down, his servants met him and told him, saying, "Your son lives!"* (John 4:50–51)

When you go deeper into these verses you can see how a short prayer can obtain healing for a loved one.

First, let's not miss Jesus' immediate willingness to heal. Some people struggle with believing that it is God's will to heal them or others. Yet we know from numerous Scriptures that Jesus was and is a perfect representation of God the Father's character and nature (Hebrews 1:3).

And Jesus Himself said that He only said those things the Father told Him to say (John 12:49–50) and only did those things He saw the Father doing (John 5:19).

So, what did Jesus demonstrate about healing throughout His ministry? Well, no one who ever approached Him for a healing miracle for themselves or a loved one came away empty-handed. Not one among the multitudes.

Nor did this man with a dying son. Could there possibly have ever been sweeter words to his ears than the Savior's response?

> *"Go your way; your son lives."* (v. 50)

Next, notice the faith that the nobleman demonstrated by obeying Jesus' instruction.

> ***"So the man believed the word that Jesus spoke to him,*** *and he went his way."* (v. 50, emphasis added)

This is the key to this man's miracle. Jesus spoke a word to him and... the man believed the word! How do we *know* that this man believed—besides the obvious fact that John tells us he did? Because of his actions!

As John reveals: *"... he went his way"* (v. 50). The father of a dying child doesn't turn and walk away unless he believes he has obtained what he came for.

The book of James tells us that faith will always be accompanied by a corresponding action (works). In fact, he declares:

For as the body without the spirit is dead, so faith without works is dead also. (James 2:26)

We see this man's faith displayed in the fact that he had traveled two days or more—uphill—just to get to Jesus. How do we know it was uphill? Because when the man headed home, John says, *"And as he was now going down..."* (v. 51).

This man had enough faith in Jesus' power and willingness to heal that he had traveled uphill, through rocky terrain, just to make his plea to Jesus. For you and me, Jesus is always and only just a breath away. Yet, so many of us neglect to take our cares and worries to Him. Sure, we may "worry" to Him. We may "complain" to Him. But do we come to Him like this man did, in faith and expectancy?

For you and me, Jesus is *always* and only just a breath away.

Yes, it is clear that this man believed Jesus' decree that his boy was healed because he instantly turned around and started back on the long, multi-day walk home. Yet, he didn't have to wait until he got there to discover the truth of Jesus' declaration. As we saw above, the next day, while he was still traveling home:

And as he was now going down, his servants met him and told him, saying, "Your son lives!" (v. 51)

Pause for a moment and think about the joy and relief this man must have felt at hearing that report. His servants who stayed behind with the deathly ill boy and his mother knew he had taken off a few days earlier on a last-ditch, desperation mission to find and request help from the healing rabbi they'd been hearing about. Then suddenly, the boy revives and is perfectly healthy! So, they instantly dispatch more men to go and find the father and give him the amazing news.

Although he probably didn't need any confirmation that it was the proclamation of Jesus that brought about the miracle, he still couldn't help but seek confirmation:

> *Then he inquired of them the hour when he got better. And they said to him, "Yesterday at the seventh hour the fever left him." So the father knew that it was at the same hour in which Jesus said to him, "Your son lives." And he himself believed, and his whole household.* (v. 52)

From that moment forward, no skeptic or doubter on earth—no matter how eloquent—could have persuaded this grateful father that Jesus of Nazareth was anyone other than who He claimed to be.

John tells us that the nobleman *"himself believed"* in Jesus, but not him alone. His *"whole household"* also believed. You see, miracles don't just impact the person who prays the short, powerful prayer. They produce a ripple effect. The man's entire sphere of influence became Jesus-believers on that day.

Here's another key truth I want you to take away from this incident. Jesus didn't have to be physically present for this man to obtain a miracle for his son. Neither faith nor God's power is constrained by the laws of space or time.

The enemy of your soul wants you to believe that if only Jesus were physically here today, you could obtain the healing your loved one needs. But this clearly isn't true.

Jesus didn't lay hands on that dying child the way he healed a man with leprosy (Mark 1:40–45) or when He opened the eyes of two blind men with a touch (Matthew 9:29–30).

No, He wasn't in the room as He was when He spoke the words *talitha koum*—"little girl rise"—to the recently deceased daughter of the synagogue official in Mark 5:41.

No, Jesus was at least a two-day journey from that child's deathbed. Yet, all He had to do was speak the word, and the boy was healed.

Those three words, *"your son lives"* (John 4:50), should put you in remembrance of the faith-filled centurion mentioned in Matthew chapter eight. There, too, we find a long-distance miracle. In that case, Jesus was ready and willing to go to a gentile Roman officer's house to heal the man's paralyzed, pain-racked servant. *"I will come and heal him,"* Jesus instantly told him (v. 7).

Here again, we see Jesus' abundant willingness to heal. But the man had such a revelation of Jesus' willingness and power that he said:

> *"Lord, I am not worthy that You should come under my roof. But only speak a word, and my servant will be healed. For I also am a man under authority, having soldiers under me. And I say to this one, 'Go,' and he goes; and to another, 'Come,' and he comes; and to my servant, 'Do this,' and he does it."* (Matthew 8:8–9)

Jesus marveled at that centurion's faith. In fact, Jesus was so impressed and blessed that He declared, *"Assuredly, I say to you, I have not found such great faith, not even in Israel!"... Then Jesus said to the centurion, "Go your way; and as you have believed, so let it be done for you." And his servant was healed that same hour* (vv. 10, 13).

Now ask yourself, *What was the specific nature of this faith that so impressed and delighted the Son of God?* It was faith that Jesus didn't need to be present to heal. It was faith that all Jesus had to do was only speak the word for miracle power to be released.

I've heard other believers make the statement, "If only I could go back to biblical times when Jesus walked the earth! If only I could touch the hem of His garment, then I know I could be healed." Jesus Christ is the same yesterday, today, and forever! Distance meant nothing back then and it means nothing now. Speaking of reaching long distances in prayer...

We've explored the faith of a father, but that doesn't mean mothers are any less capable of obtaining a miracle for a loved one. If anything, praying mothers are often the mightiest intercessors in the church. That truth reminds me of a true story I heard years ago.

In 1820, a man named Peter Richley stepped aboard a ship in England, bound for Australia. He couldn't have known that he was about to become living proof of what happens when a mother refuses to release her hold on Heaven's promises for a son or daughter.

The ship sank in a violent storm. Everyone perished except Peter, who found himself alone in the vast ocean, bobbing up and down on the massive, wind-driven waves. Trapped in a tug of war between the sky and the sea, between life and death. But eventually, miraculously, a second ship appeared.

Rescued from the depths, Peter must have felt relief beyond description. At least until the same raging storm also sank the ship that rescued him.

And then a third rescuing vessel.

And a fourth.

And a fifth!

Five times death reached for him. Five times an invisible but powerful force said, "Not yet!" The ocean tried five times to take what God wanted to keep safe.

Can you imagine the questions swirling in Peter's heart? Why was he under such attack? And, also, why was he being saved? What force kept pushing back the hand of death?

When a sixth ship—the *City of Leeds*—pulled him from the frigid waters, Peter was about to discover the answer to those questions.

The captain approached him with an unusual request. Below deck lay a dying woman, an elderly mother whose kindness and godliness had captured every heart on board. In her fever, they had heard her pray one specific prayer over and over:

"Oh God, let me see my son one more time!"

Hoping to provide some comfort to a sweet, dying woman, the captain asked Peter to pretend to be her son. He hoped to provide a little peace and comfort to her in her final moments. But when Peter entered that cabin and looked upon that frail, silver-haired saint lying there, he fell to his knees weeping.

He had no need to pretend. It was Sarah Richley—his own mother, whom he hadn't seen in ten years.

Do you see it? Every shipwreck and rescue was the hand of God redirecting his path in response to a mother's fervent prayer. Every rescue was Heaven responding to a mother's unshakeable faith. Sarah Richley's prayers created a force field of protection that Hell itself could not penetrate.

This is what I need you to understand about your own prayers for healing, for breakthrough, for your loved ones: You are not just speaking words into the air. You are releasing the very power of Heaven into situations that look impossible.

Sarah didn't know her son was drowning five times over. She didn't need to know the details. She just needed to know the heart of God—and she refused to let go.

You are not just speaking words into the air. You are *releasing* the very power of Heaven into situations that look impossible.

Pondering the power of a praying mother reminds me of my grandmother, Lettie.

For most of her life she lived outside a little town called Middlesex in the piney woods east of Raleigh, North Carolina. She and my grandfather raised eighteen children in their home. That's not a misprint. *Eighteen* children. My mother was one of them.

Grandma Lettie had gone home to be with the Lord long before I was born, but she left our family a wonderful legacy of faith. My mom describes her as one of the greatest saints in her life and said she genuinely lived for the Lord. Every night Lettie would take as many children as she could wrap her arms around and love and pray for them.

Over the years, our family would visit her childhood home. Even though the house had indoor plumbing there was an outhouse on the property, like most families in rural America back then.

This outhouse however, was unique. It was covered inside with prayers and scriptures Grandma Lettie would write if she felt like one of the children were going through a struggle or something wasn't going right in their life.

It seems that with that many kids in the house, finding some quiet time to get with God and pray was nearly impossible to come by. So apparently, when she needed to pray, she'd make time to visit the outhouse and turn it into her prayer closet.

There, amid the only solitude she could find, Lettie would inscribe her requests and pour out her heart to God and put Him in remembrance of His Word. One of my relatives recalls seeing one particular prayer written on the wall. It read:

> August 6, 1948, The baby is sick. Maybe it won't amount to much. Polio is spreading. Lord, keep her and protect her. And help us to be more humble, more obedient, more bold, and more spiritual.

The scourge of polio did not, could not, come near her dwelling.

I remember being a kid and looking at the things written on those walls. It was an amazing thing to see what my grandmother had been talking to God about decades before I was born.

Grandma Lettie passed away peacefully when she was only 39. Eventually Grandpa Stone remarried another powerful woman of God, Thelma. Together, they added an additional 10 children to the family. That's 28 children in all!

Thelma was the only grandmother I knew during my childhood, and I will always remember her praying for me and all the grandchildren. She was a prayer warrior.

Her prayers played a crucial role in guiding me to embrace God's calling for my life.

Unknowingly, both of these remarkable women wove a shield of protection around our family through their prayers. I am merely one part of their enduring legacy of faith. My children and grandchildren now share in this legacy as well. Their short prayers secured miracles for many they loved, just as the nobleman's brief prayer brought healing to his son.

A key lesson from these stories is that a miracle for someone you care about doesn't depend on that person having faith. Did the nobleman's son have faith that Jesus would heal him? The dying boy probably didn't even know that his father was seeking Jesus' help! Did the centurion's servant have faith in Jesus for a long-distance miracle? The Word doesn't even hint at this.

No, both the nobleman and the centurion obtained a healing miracle for someone they cared about, and in both cases they simply believed in the word Jesus spoke.

The same can be true of you and me today. We can still go to the Bible or go to our prayer closets and get a word from Jesus. The question is, having received that word, what will we do with it?

There is one final lesson I want you to take from the nobleman and his seven-word prayer. There's a truth hidden in a little detail in verse 52 of that passage. It's necessary to look at a few other translations to see it clearly. For example, here is that verse in the King James Version:

> *Then enquired he of them the hour* ***when he began to amend.*** *And they said unto him, Yesterday at the seventh hour the fever left him.*

"Amend" is King James English for *improve*. Here is that verse in the New American Standard Version:

> *So, he inquired of them the hour when* ***he began to get better***. *Then they said to him, "Yesterday at the seventh hour the fever left him."*

What these translations and others suggest is that this boy's healing wasn't instantaneous. It was progressive. In other words, the very hour Jesus spoke the word and the father, believing it, headed home, was the moment the boy began to get better.

His healing miracle was gradual. Incremental. Progressive.

Some healings come like lightning! Others come like the dawn—gradually pushing back darkness until full light appears (Proverbs 4:18). But both are equally miraculous! Both demonstrate God's power!

You may have prayed a prayer for healing (short or long) and still don't feel anything different today. The doctor's report might not change tomorrow. But that doesn't mean God hasn't already set healing in motion! From the moment you believe His Word, recovery begins!

Some *healings* come like lightning! Others come like the dawn—gradually pushing back darkness until full light appears.

I've seen progressive, gradual healing on countless occasions in my life and ministry.

The very same power, the same willingness, the same Jesus that spoke the word to that nobleman is available to you right now.

I understand that some people pray for physical healing and do not receive it in the way they expect. Yet, God remains sovereign, and in His perfect timing, He brings healing to all, whether in this life or the next. Like the three Hebrew boys in Daniel 3, we must hold fast to an unshakable trust that God knows what is best. Even if His response differs from our hopes, we will continue to serve Him faithfully.

Your Short Prayer:

Jesus, my loved one needs restoration and healing. I have Your words and Your Word. I receive them in confident faith and expectancy.

CHAPTER 12

When You Need Victory Over the Enemy

A 9-Word Prayer

So it was, whenever the ark set out, that Moses said: ***"Rise up, O Lord! Let Your enemies be scattered,*** *and let those who hate You flee before You."*
(NUMBERS 10:35)

It seems Israel has always faced enemies. It's true today, and it was true thirty-five centuries ago.

It's also true that God has always promised His people victory over their enemies when they're walking out His plans and purposes. It was true for His people during their wilderness journey. And it's true for you and me as we journey through the wilderness of this fallen, broken world.

In the tenth chapter of the book of Numbers, we see that God specifically instructed Moses to pray the nine-word prayer highlighted in verse 35 every time they pulled up stakes to move into a new spot in the wilderness.

Whenever it was time to move into new territory, the glory cloud that rested on the Tabernacle's Holy Place would lift and become a pillar of cloud by day and fire by night that led them to the next place to camp.

And it seemed that whenever the twelve tribes moved to a new place, there were new enemies waiting to oppose and threaten them. Which is why God gave Moses this request to speak on moving day:

"Rise up, O LORD! Let your enemies be scattered..."

As Numbers chapter 10 reveals, whenever the cloud moved, the first thing to happen was the Levites would disassemble the Tabernacle—the heart of which was the Holy Place and the Most Holy Place (or holy of holies.) And in the holy of holies sat the ark of the covenant. All of which had been designed in accordance with God's instructions down to the tiniest detail.

That gold-clad wooden box with angelic figures on its lid was the most significant item on planet earth. Inside were three power-packed, supernatural reminders of God's faithfulness:

1. The golden pot of manna that reminded them God provides supernaturally.

2. The stone tablets of the Law that reminded them God gives victory through His Word.

3. Aaron's rod that budded—a dry staff that supernaturally blossomed to remind them of God's power to bring life from death.

The ark and the glory cloud represented God's presence among His people. So when the ark rested, they camped. When the ark moved, they followed. And when it moved toward enemies who stood in their way, Moses would pray: *"Rise up, O Lord! Let your enemies be scattered."*

Those nine words were to be spoken as the ark of the covenant moved out to lead the way into battle. It stands as one of the most powerful warfare prayers in Scripture.

But this prayer is just as relevant today as it was 3,500 years ago. It reveals a profound spiritual principle for you and me. Namely, when God arises, His enemies don't just retreat—they are scattered, defeated, and put to flight. Picture a lion running toward a flock of pigeons on the ground, and you get the general idea.

If you're facing battles that seem too big for you to handle, if enemies from Hell are coming against your family, your health, your finances, or your peace, you need to understand the spiritual power contained in Moses' ancient battle cry. Because the same God who scattered Israel's enemies is ready to arise on your behalf today.

When God *arises*, His enemies don't just retreat—they are scattered, defeated, and put to flight.

As born-again believers, we carry the glory of God in us just as the ark of the covenant did. That's why Paul speaks of *"Christ in you, the hope of glory"* (Colossians 1:27). And it's why he asks, *"Do you not know that you are God's temple and that God's Spirit dwells in you?"* (1 Corinthians 3:16, ESV).

To understand the full power of Moses' prayer, we need to picture the scene in the wilderness of Sinai. The children of Israel weren't just wandering aimlessly around the desert—they were following the very presence of God Himself, represented by the holy ark of the covenant.

Here's what I want you to see in this. God had two modes of operation for His people. Sometimes He was at rest—settling down in that sweet, powerful peace that only He can give. But other times, God was rising up—moving in great glory and power to take new territory and drive out alien armies.

The phrase *"let your enemies be scattered"* literally means "let them be shattered into pieces." This wasn't just about winning a battle—it was about complete and total victory over every force that opposed God's people.

When battles came, God had a specific battle plan. The first instruction was always the same: "Send Judah up first." Judah was the tribe whose name means "praise" in Hebrew. The tribe of Judah always camped on the eastern side of the camp—the side that greets the rising morning sun.

This was no coincidence. Ancient Hebrew priests and teachers understood that when God shows up, He comes from the east. That's why Solomon built the Temple facing due east. That's why even Jonah, in the belly of the whale, remembered the temple in his prayer to the Lord (Jonah 2).

When God arises, He comes like the sunrise—not with gloom and doom, but with light and victory. The prophet Malachi foresaw the day Jesus would come and wrote:

> *"But to you who fear My name the Sun of Righteousness shall arise with healing in His wings; and you shall go out and grow fat like stall-fed calves."* (Malachi 4:2)

Yes, the life-giving sun represents God's presence. And who gets His presence first? The praising people, represented by the tribe of Judah! The people who understand that worship isn't just something you do in church—it's a weapon of warfare that activates God's power against every enemy.

This reveals something crucial about spiritual warfare: God doesn't just want us to ask Him to rise up against our enemies. He wants us to create an atmosphere of praise and worship that welcomes His presence and activates His power.

The ark of the covenant has been missing for about 2,800 years. That means it wasn't in Herod's temple when Jesus walked the earth. Scholars debate what happened to it, but Scripture reveals why it is not likely to be found.

In Jesus' final moments on the cross, he cried out, *"It is finished!"* (John 19:30). At that instant the thick veil blocking access to the holy of holies in the temple was torn from top to bottom (Matthew 27:51). This was God's declaration that His manifest presence and glory on earth were no longer confined behind a curtain in a small space.

Instead, because of the redemptive work Jesus accomplished on the cross, God's glory and power would reside in the hearts of His people. That's why 1 Corinthians 6:19 declares, *"Or do you not know that your body is the temple of the Holy Spirit who is in you, whom you have from God, and you are not your own?"*

When Jesus walked into the synagogue in Luke 4:18 (ESV) and declared, *"The Spirit of the Lord is upon me,"* the demons suddenly realized: "The ark is back! After 2,800 years, there it is! The box is that Man!" Jesus wasn't just carrying God's presence—He WAS God's presence in human form. He was *Immanuel*—"God with us!"

And now, through His Spirit living in us, we carry that same supernatural presence. The manna (salvation), the Law (sanctification), and Aaron's budding rod (the power of the Holy Spirit) all reside within every believer.

Here's where Moses' prayer becomes intensely practical for you and me today. Just as the Old Testament tabernacle had three courts—the outer court, the inner court, and the holy of holies—so we have three aspects to our being: body, soul, and spirit (1 Thessalonians 5:23).

And just as there were entry points, or gates, that had to be opened to access each court of the tabernacle, there are gates we must open to access the fullness of God's power to bring victory in our lives.

1. The Mouth Gate.

Ecclesiastes 5:6 warns us not to let our mouths cause our flesh to sin, but the positive truth is equally powerful: when we open our mouths in praise, we open the gateway to God's presence.

This is why David wrote, *"Enter into his gates with thanksgiving, and into his courts with praise. Be thankful to Him, and bless His name"* (Psalm 100:4). You cannot access the supernatural realm with your mouth shut. If you want God to arise against your enemies, you must first open the gate of praise.

Too many Christians sit in church like "knots on a log," expecting God to move while they contribute nothing but their physical presence. But praise isn't optional—it's the key that unlocks the first gate to God's presence and power.

> **Praise isn't optional—it's the *key* that unlocks the first gate to God's presence and power.**

When you're facing impossible situations, don't just pray quietly. Open your mouth and begin to praise God audibly. Declare His goodness, His faithfulness, His power. When the praises go up, God comes down. No exceptions.

2. The Eye Gate.

In Matthew 6:22–23, Jesus brings us an important and sobering truth:

> *"The lamp of the body is the eye. If therefore your eye is good, your whole body will be full of light. But if your eye is bad, your whole body will be full of darkness. If therefore the light that is in you is darkness, how great is that darkness!"*

Let me put that another way. What you choose to look at determines what fills your inner being. This gate influences your will, your emotions, your mind—what Scripture calls your soul. If you fill your eyes with corruption, fear, and negativity, your whole inner being becomes dark.

But if you focus your eyes on Jesus, on His promises, on His faithfulness, light floods your soul.

This is more than positive thinking—it's spiritual warfare! When enemies are coming against you, you must choose what you're going to focus on. Will you stare at the size of your problems, or will you fix your eyes on the might, glory, and faithfulness of your heavenly Father?

3. The Ear Gate.

This one is perhaps the most important of all. Why? Because Romans 10:17 tells us that *"faith comes by hearing, and hearing by the word of God."* This gate opens directly into your spirit—your personal holy of holies where God dwells within you.

When God wants to give you something supernatural, it comes through your ear into your spirit. You'll be sitting in church, and suddenly you'll hear God speak a word directly to your heart. The person next to you might be bored, but you're thinking, *Oh my! I just had something downloaded to me from Heaven!*

That word from God opens the gate to everything you need. It opens the gate to your healing, your breakthrough, your miracle. When you "hear" a word from God in your spirit, suddenly you have access to supernatural power that can defeat any enemy.

Here's where Moses' prayer becomes even more powerful. The lid of the ark of the covenant was called the mercy seat. And Scripture tells us a sobering story about what happened when that lid was opened in the wrong way.

In 1 Samuel 5, we learn that when the Philistines captured the ark, diseases and plagues broke out among them, so they desperately tried to return it. They quickly learned that the power meant to be a blessing to Israel was a curse to them. Later, when some Israelites carelessly lifted the lid out of curiosity, over 50,000 people died as a result (1 Samuel 6:19).

But here's the takeaway lesson: when God arises in power, His enemies are scattered. There's enough power in God's presence to destroy cancer, to shatter depression, to demolish addiction, and to defeat every demon that comes against your family.

There's enough *power* in God's presence to destroy cancer, to shatter depression, to demolish addiction, and to defeat every demon that comes against your family.

The key is learning how to open the gates properly and invite God to arise. When, in faith, you worship with your mouth, focus with your eyes, and receive with your ears, you create an atmosphere where God can lift the lid on His supernatural power.

Here's something crucial to understand: God doesn't struggle against your enemies. Satan is not an equal opponent giving God a hard time. When God arises, the battle is over before it begins.

Too often we act as though God and the devil are in some kind of cosmic wrestling match over our situations. That's an insult to God's power. The devil is a defeated foe, and when God stands up, every enemy scatters like leaves in a hurricane.

This is why it's so important to lift God up in praise and worship. When you magnify Him—when you make Him big in your perspective—His enemies don't stand a chance.

Remember, you don't have to wait for a church service or a special meeting to access this power. Today, the ark of the covenant lives inside you. The presence of God that causes enemies to flee in terror is residing in your spirit right now.

When you wake up in the morning facing battles, you can give voice to Moses' prayer out loud: *"Rise up, O Lord! Let your enemies be scattered."*

When cancer tries to attack your body, when depression attempts to overwhelm your mind, when financial pressure seeks to destroy your peace—you have the authority to declare God's arising against every enemy.

Just remember the pattern. Praise goes first. Open the mouth gate, then the eye gate, and then the ear gate. Create a spiritual atmosphere in you and around you where God can arise in power. And whatever you do, don't try to fight your battles in your own strength. Instead, invite the God of supernatural victory to rise up on your behalf.

In Acts chapter 2, the Holy Spirit was poured out on the day of Pentecost. But notice something significant. Nowhere does Scripture say He ever went back up. That means we're not waiting for Him to fall—He's waiting for us to open the gates and let Him arise.

The Holy Spirit is here among us and in us right now, ready to move in supernatural power. The question isn't whether He's able or willing to defeat your enemies. The question is whether you're willing to open the gates and invite Him to arise.

When you learn to access God's presence through praise, focus, and faith, you tap into a realm that's as real as the physical world around you. Angels are ready to back up God's Word. Supernatural power is available to those who know how to enter in.

Here's the truth that will revolutionize your spiritual life. You decide what kind of victory you're going to experience. Not the preacher, not the worship team, not anyone else. YOU determine whether you're going to open the gates and invite God to arise.

You can sit on the sidelines, watching others experience breakthrough while you remain locked out. Or you can humble yourself, open your mouth in praise, fix your eyes on Jesus, open your ears to His Word, and watch God arise against every enemy in your life.

There are no shortcuts around the gates. You can't sneak into God's presence through the back door. But when you're willing to follow His Word-ordained pattern—when you send Judah (praise) first, when you honor His presence, when you create an atmosphere of worship and faith—He will arise with such power that every enemy will scatter.

The power of this prayer isn't in its length or complexity—it's in the recognition that our God is the God of supernatural victory. When He arises, enemies don't just retreat—they are scattered, shattered, and put to flight.

Today, whatever battles you're facing, remember that you carry the ark of the covenant within you. Open the gates, invite God to arise, and watch Him scatter every enemy that has dared to come against what belongs to Him.

Your Short Prayer:

Rise up, Lord, and let Your enemies be scattered! I open the gates of my mouth in praise, my eyes in focus on You, and my ears to hear Your Word. Arise with Your supernatural power against every force that comes against me and my family. Let Your enemies flee before You!

CHAPTER 13

When You Wonder if God Sees Your Tears

A 28-Word Prayer

Then Hezekiah turned his face toward the wall, and prayed to the Lord, and said, ***"Remember now, O Lord, I pray, how I have walked before You in truth and with a loyal heart, and have done what is good in Your sight."*** *And Hezekiah wept bitterly.*

(ISAIAH 38:2–3)

These words, spoken through tears by a king who was dying, stand as one of the most honest and vulnerable prayers recorded in Scripture.

King Hezekiah of Judah wasn't asking God to remember some big theological accomplishment or impressive religious achievement. He wasn't pointing to any personal success. No. In his darkest hour, facing a death sentence from both disease and divine decree, he simply asked God to remember his faithfulness—and then he wept bitterly.

But here's what makes this prayer so remarkable: God not only heard those words, He saw every tear. And those tears moved the heart of the Almighty. Hezekiah has surely read the words his royal ancestor David had penned in Psalm 56:8:

> *You number my wanderings; put my tears in Your bottle; are they not in Your book?*

Here David assures us that God records every tear we've ever shed. He doesn't just take note of our pain—He collects it, is moved by it, and responds to it.

God not only heard those words, He saw every tear. And those tears *moved the heart* of the Almighty.

If you've ever wondered whether God sees your tears, whether He notices your pain, whether your broken heart matters to Him—this psalm combined with God's response to Hezekiah's prayer holds your answer. Because the same God who collected David's tears in His bottle is collecting yours today.

We'll examine that response shortly, but first let's get a clearer picture of Hezekiah's situation. The scene opens with devastating news. King Hezekiah, in the prime of his reign, receives a visit from the prophet Isaiah with the most sobering message anyone could hear: "*Set your house in order, for you shall die and not live*" (Isaiah 38:1). Imagine receiving that telegram from Heaven. No hope for recovery. No possibility of healing. Just a direct word from God Himself: your time is up.

But notice Hezekiah's response. He didn't argue with the prophet. He didn't demand a second opinion. He didn't rage against God or question His justice. Instead, he turned his face toward the wall—away from the prophet, away from the people around him, away from anyone who might witness his vulnerability—and he poured out his heart to God.

This teaches us something important about prayer in crisis moments. Sometimes the most powerful prayers happen when we turn away from human comfort and human solutions and face God alone with our pain and fears.

Now note the content of Hezekiah's prayer. In that moment, he prayed, *"Remember now, O Lord, I pray, how I have walked before You in truth and with a loyal heart, and have done what is good in Your sight"* (v. 3).

At first glance, this might seem presumptuous. Prideful even. After all, who are we to remind God of anything? And God is a better judge of our behavior than we are ourselves. But Hezekiah wasn't being arrogant—he was being desperate. And in his desperation, he appealed to the one thing he knew might move God's heart: a life lived in faithful service.

What exactly was Hezekiah reminding God of? The Scriptures reveal three specific things that marked his reign and his relationship with God.

First: Hezekiah reopened the doors of God's house. Second Chronicles 29:3 tells us that *"in the first year of his reign, in the first month, [he] opened the doors of the house of the Lord and repaired them."* You see, when Hezekiah became king, he found the temple closed, abandoned, and in disrepair. His first act as king wasn't to build a palace or expand his military—it was to restore worship to the land.

This wasn't done out of religious duty. This act revealed the priorities of his heart. Hezekiah seemed to understand that nothing in his kingdom would prosper until God's house was restored to its proper place. He put God's house first, and God remembered that.

Second: Hezekiah restored true worship. That same chapter in 2 Chronicles reveals that Hezekiah *"commanded the Levites to sing praise to the* L*ORD* *with the words of David and of Asaph the seer. So they sang praise with gladness, and they bowed their heads and worshiped"* (2 Chronicles 29:30).

Hezekiah didn't just open the doors—he filled the house with praise. He understood that God inhabits the praises of His people, and he made sure that authentic worship flowed from the temple once again. Even in his prayer, he reminded God, *"The living, the living man, he shall praise You"* (Isaiah 38:19). He was basically saying, "If I die, You'll lose a praiser in the earth. Only the living can offer You praise on this planet."

Third: Hezekiah restored sacrificial giving. Second Chronicles 29 describes how Hezekiah reinstituted the offerings and sacrifices prescribed by the Levitical laws. The people brought hundreds of animals as burnt offerings and consecrated sacrifices. In the following chapter, during the Passover celebration in one offering alone, he brought 1,000 bulls and 7,000 sheep. This wasn't just a religious ceremony—this was sacrificial giving that demonstrated his heartfelt repentance and love toward God.

When Hezekiah faced death, these were the three things he reminded God of: his commitment to God's house, his heart of worship, and his sacrificial giving. Not his bloodline or ancestors, not his military victories, not his wealth, not his political achievements—but his faithfulness in the fundamentals of relationship with God.

But here's what moves me most about this story. After Hezekiah finished his prayer, he "... *wept bitterly*" (v. 3).

The Hebrew word translated "wept" here is an intense one. It means to weep aloud, to cry with deep, gut-wrenching sobs. This wasn't a few tears rolling down his cheeks—this was the kind of weeping that comes from the depths of a broken heart.

And God saw every tear. As we've already noted, David declared in the 56th psalm that God collects our tears in a bottle. There's something about tears that moves the heart of God in a way that even eloquent words cannot. When our hearts are so broken that words fail us, our tears become a language that Heaven understands perfectly.

God's response to Hezekiah's prayer was swift and sweet. Before Isaiah could even leave the palace grounds, God stopped him and gave him a new message: *"Go and tell Hezekiah, Thus says the Lord, the God of David your father: 'I have heard your prayer, I have seen your tears; surely* ***I will add to your days fifteen years****'"* (Isaiah 38:5). What a glorious response from our gracious Father.

When our hearts are so broken that words fail us, our tears become a language that Heaven understands perfectly.

On numerous occasions in my life and ministry, the Holy Ghost has brought this miracle to mind when a friend or loved one has gotten a devastating report at the doctor's office. And on those occasions when the diagnosis was "terminal" and the report was "no hope"—I've brought this incident to the Lord's remembrance. I've asked God to *"Do it again! Give this person at least fifteen more years!"* and on numerous occasions, we've seen a miracle. *"Remission." "Unexplainable recovery."*

Notice the contents of God's reply: *"I have heard your prayer, I have seen your tears..."* God didn't just hear Hezekiah's words—He saw his pain. The tears weren't separate from the prayer; they were part of it. They were the exclamation point that emphasized the sincerity of his heart.

But God didn't stop with healing. He gave Hezekiah a confirming sign that defied the laws of nature: He made the shadow on the palace sundial go backward ten degrees. For one man's prayer and tears, the God who spoke the stars and planets into existence interfered with the rotation of the earth itself. The entire universe paused and reversed to demonstrate that He had heard and responded to a broken heart.

This episode in Hezekiah's life gives us a great opportunity to contrast life in the old covenant versus life in the new. Hezekiah's grant of an extra fifteen years took place in the heart of the old covenant period. And yes, God is the same yesterday, today, and forever. But there are some wonderful differences for you and me today.

Back under the old covenant, Hezekiah's approach to God for favor and blessing came with the need to show he was doing all the "good works" the Law required. In other words, he came to God flashing his spiritual credentials and citing his accomplishments. It was a works-based appeal. That was the appropriate approach under the old covenant.

But for you and me, our connection to God under the new covenant changes prayer from a "works-based appeal" to "grace-based access." You and I don't need perfect credentials to get a supernatural intervention from Heaven. Grace qualifies us for miracles.

In other words, when you're facing a terminal diagnosis or some other "impossible" situation, you're in a far better position before God's throne than Hezekiah could have been on his best day.

Grace qualifies us for *miracles*.

This story connects to a broader truth that runs throughout Scripture: God is for you, not against you. Even when circumstances seem to declare otherwise, even when multiple problems pile up at once, even when you feel like the whole world is conspiring against you—God is for you.

Consider Jacob's story. He faced a worldwide famine, believed his son Joseph was dead, had another son, Simeon, imprisoned in Egypt, and felt overwhelmed by circumstances beyond his control. *"All these things are against me"* he cried (Genesis 42:36).

But what Jacob didn't know was that Joseph—his supposedly dead son—was alive and ruling Egypt. Joseph was the one controlling the very situation that Jacob was wailing about. The son he thought he had lost was in charge, working everything together for good.

This is a picture of our Savior, Jesus. When everything seems to be going wrong, when tears flow and hearts break, when we feel abandoned and forgotten—Jesus is alive and seated at the right hand of the Father, controlling the very circumstances that threaten to overwhelm us.

The same God who heard Hezekiah's prayer and saw his tears is the God who "is for you." Romans 8:31 declares, *"If God is for us, who can be against us?"* This is the heart of the heavenly Father toward His children.

Perhaps you're reading this through your own tears. Maybe you've received devastating news, are facing impossible circumstances, or feel the crushing weight of problems that seem too heavy to bear. Maybe you've wondered if God sees your pain, if He cares about your struggles, if your tears matter to Him.

The answer is found in Hezekiah's story and echoed throughout Scripture: God sees every tear, hears every prayer, and responds to every broken heart that cries out to Him in truth.

Your tears aren't a sign of weakness—they're a language that Heaven understands. They're not evidence that God has abandoned you—they're proof that you're still fighting, still believing, still hoping that the God who created the universe cares about your individual pain.

David wrote, *"When I cry out to You, then my enemies will turn back; this I know, because God is for me"* (Psalm 56:9). There's something about the cry of a broken heart that activates Heaven's response. When you cry out to God, He doesn't just hear your words—He sees your tears, and your enemies must turn back because God is for you.

Here's what amazes me most about Hezekiah's story: God didn't just heal him—He reversed His own prophetic word. Through Isaiah, God had declared that Hezekiah would die. But one prayer, accompanied by bitter tears from a faithful heart, caused God to change His mind and add fifteen years to the king's life.

This reveals something profound about the heart of God. He's not bound by our circumstances, our diagnoses, our limitations, or even His own previous declarations. When genuine faith meets desperate need, when tears flow from hearts that have walked faithfully before Him, God can and will intervene in ways that defy natural law.

The same God who turned back the shadow on the sundial for Hezekiah is the God who sees your tears today. He's not limited by medical reports, financial statements, or human opinions. He's the God of supernatural reversal, and He specializes in turning impossible situations around.

Your Short Prayer:

Lord, You know my heart. You see my tears. You understand my pain. I have tried to walk before You in truth, to worship You with gladness, to give sacrificially of what You've blessed me with. In this moment of crisis, I ask You to remember my faithfulness and respond to my broken heart. You are for me, not against me, and I trust You to work all things together for my good.

CHAPTER 14

When You Need a Pattern for Praying

A 66-Word Prayer

"In this manner, therefore, pray: ***Our Father in heaven, hallowed be Your name. Your kingdom come. Your will be done on earth as it is in heaven. Give us this day our daily bread. And forgive us our debts, as we forgive our debtors. And do not lead us into temptation, but deliver us from the evil one. For Yours is the kingdom and the power and the glory forever. Amen."***
(MATTHEW 6:9–13)

"Whenever I take time to pray, I don't know what to say." "I don't even know how to pray about this situation!" "When I try to pray, my mind just wanders all over the place."

I've talked to countless believers over the years who have made statements similar to the ones above. Whenever I hear them, I always have good news to share. Jesus Himself has given us a pattern—a roadmap or blueprint—for praying.

Jesus! You can't get a higher source than that. What we call the Lord's Prayer was simply Jesus responding to a request from His disciples, *"Lord, teach us to pray..."* (Luke 11:1). What if there is undiscovered gold for us in His answer? I know there is.

For more than thirty years, I've prayed through the Lord's Prayer almost every day. And I've discovered that there's nothing more powerful than praying back to God what He's already told us to pray.

But it's not just a set of words to memorize and recite by repetition. No. It's a framework. It's a map. A path to walk. And when we follow the path of the Lord's Prayer, we're entering into the very heart of God through the pattern His Son gave us.

This prayer pattern contains everything we need to make a transformational connection to Heaven: worship, surrender, provision, forgiveness, protection, and victory.

Intimacy and Awe

The first few words are very powerful: *"Our Father in heaven..."*

It's difficult for us to understand how scandalous and shocking it was when Jesus showed up in first-century Israel referring to God as "my Father." Observant Jews of that day didn't even dare speak or write the sacred Hebrew name of God— יְהוָה—YHWH (Yahweh).

Jewish scribes added *Adonai* vowels to YHWH to cue reading *Adonai* instead of pronouncing the name of God. Medieval Christians later misread this, creating the familiar name "Jehovah."

And yet Jesus walked onto the scene referring to the Most High God as "Father!" Take a look at this passage from the fifth chapter of John:

> *For this reason the Jews persecuted Jesus, and sought to kill Him, because He had done these things on the Sabbath. But Jesus answered them, "**My Father** has been working until now, and I have been working." Therefore the Jews sought all the more to kill Him, because He not only broke the Sabbath, but also said that God was His Father, making Himself equal with God.*
> (John 5:16–18, emphasis added)

It was one thing for Him—the Son of Man, the Son of God, divinity in human flesh—to call God "Father." But when asked about prayer, He instructed regular Jesus followers like you and me to call God our Father, too!

When Jesus taught us to begin our prayers with *"Our Father,"* He was revealing something stunning. The God who spoke galaxies into existence, who holds the stars in His hands, who commands the forces of nature—this same God wants us to approach Him not as distant subjects before a remote king, but as beloved children coming to their Father.

But notice that Jesus said, *"Our Father in heaven."* He isn't suggesting that we approach the God of the universe with a casual familiarity that forgets who God is. But He is suggesting that we have access to an intimate relationship that remembers exactly who God is while still coming *"boldly to the throne of grace, that we may obtain mercy and find grace to help in time of need"* (Hebrews 4:16).

Also please note that He's *our* Father, pointing us to the reality that in Jesus' Kingdom, none of us is an only child. None of us is an island. We all belong to something bigger than ourselves—the global Church, the Body of Christ. We belong to a family and are made to live out this Christian life in community.

But He's not just our Father. He's our Father *in Heaven*—the One whose throne is surrounded by extraordinary living creatures. *"Each of the four living creatures had six wings and was covered with eyes all around, even under its wings. Day and night they never stop saying: 'Holy, holy, holy is the Lord God Almighty,' who was, and is, and is to come"* (Revelation 4:8, NIV).

This balance of awe and intimacy changes everything about prayer. We come boldly because He's our Father. We come reverently because He's in Heaven. We come confidently because we're His children. We come humbly because He's the Almighty.

Before you can approach God as Father, you need to appreciate how this relationship became possible. It was no small thing. It cost everything. When Jesus laid His life down on that cross, His blood purchased your adoption into God's family. So as you begin to pray, picture Calvary. See the cross. Thank God that you can call Him Father by virtue of the blood of Jesus Christ.

We come *reverently* because He's in Heaven. We come *confidently* because we're His children.

Worship

This is why the Lord's Prayer then takes us to worship. When you take in the magnitude of what the Father and the Son had to do to redeem you, worship is the only appropriate response.

This is why the next part of this prayer is *"hallowed be Your name."*

The word "hallowed" means to reverence, to set apart as holy, to honor with the deepest respect. Before we ask for anything, we acknowledge who God is and what He means to us. And in the pattern Jesus gave us, it is God's *name* that we hallow.

When we hallow God's name, we're doing more than showing respect—we're reminding ourselves of His character and His covenant promises. A powerful way to do that is to become familiar with the names of God that appear in the Old Testament. Those names represent every need we have in life, and when we hallow those names, we're declaring our faith in who He is and what He provides. Let's explore some of those names.

Jehovah Tsidkenu: The Lord Our Righteousness—When we hallow this name, we're thanking God that our sins are forgiven, that we stand in right relationship with Him not because of our performance but because of Christ's sacrifice. When pondering this name, it's appropriate to say, "I thank You that I am the righteousness of God in Christ Jesus. I thank You that I am forgiven, cleansed, and called Your child."

Jehovah Shalom: The Lord Our Peace—When we hallow this name, we're receiving God's peace that passes understanding. Declare, "I receive Your peace in my home, in my family, in every decision and transition. You are not mad at me. Through the cross, You have given peace on earth and goodwill toward men."

Jehovah Shammah: The Lord Who Is There—When we hallow this name, we're acknowledging God's abiding presence. In response to this revelation, you can proclaim, "You never leave me or forsake me. You are with me as my healer, my deliverer, my present help in trouble. Nothing can separate me from Your love."

Jehovah Rapha: The Lord Who Heals—When we hallow this name, we're declaring God's power over sickness and disease. This is the time to declare, "By Your stripes I am healed. You are the God who heals the lepers, opens blind eyes, and causes the lame to leap. I speak health and healing in Your mighty name."

Jehovah Jireh: The Lord Will Provide—When we hallow this name, we're trusting God as our source of provision. In faith and expectancy declare, "My God shall supply all my needs according to His riches in glory. You will open the windows of Heaven and pour out blessings I won't have room to receive."

Jehovah Nissi: The Lord My Banner—When we hallow this name, we're claiming God's protection and victory. Say, "You are my refuge and fortress. A thousand may fall at my side, but it shall not come near me. You give Your angels charge over me to keep me in all my ways."

If you can't remember all the individual names, remember this: God has highly exalted Jesus and given Him a name that is above every name. In the name of Jesus is healing, provision, righteousness, peace, presence, and protection. When you hallow the name of Jesus, you're invoking every blessing and benefit that belongs to God's children.

Surrender

The next item on the pattern Jesus provided for us comes in the phrase *"Your kingdom come. Your will be done on earth as it is in heaven."*

Why? Because after worship comes surrender. This is where we align our hearts with God's heart, where we submit our desires to His perfect plan.

This is where we pray for ourselves and our families. Name your loved ones as you pray. "Lord, Your will be done in my marriage, in my children, in my relationships. More than I want them to have money and things, I want them to know You, love You, and honor You."

At this point we pray for our churches and our pastors. "Lord, bless the church and ministries You've called me to support. Use them to reach the lost and build Your Kingdom."

This is where we pray for our nation and our world. "Lord, it's not Your will that any should perish but that all should come to repentance. Give us leaders who will seek You and honor Your Word. Bring revival to our land. Heal our nation."

Here's an opportunity for us to pray for the lost and broken. "Lord, break the chains of addiction, sexual bondage, and spiritual darkness. Set the captives free and bring them into Your Kingdom."

The beautiful thing about praying *"Your will be done"* is that we're not trying to convince God to do something He doesn't want to do. We're asking Him to do what He already wants to do—to establish His Kingdom, to save the lost, to heal the broken, to restore what's been damaged.

> **The beautiful thing about praying *"Your will be done"* is that we're not trying to convince God to do something He doesn't want to do. We're asking Him to do what He already wants to do.**

Petition

After worship and surrender comes petition. *"Give us this day our daily bread."* This is where we ask God to meet our practical, daily needs. And notice that Jesus included this in the prayer—God cares about our material needs, not just our spiritual ones.

At this moment we pray for our finances, our businesses, our employment. "Lord, prosper the work of my hands. Give me favor in the marketplace. Open doors no man can shut. Provide creative ideas and wise investments."

Right here we pray for breakthrough and provision. "Lord, You said You would rebuke the devourer for our sake. Break the curse of poverty off our families. Release supernatural provision from unexpected sources."

This is the time we declare our trust in God's goodness. "Lord, You're not against me—You're for me. You take pleasure in the prosperity of Your children. I don't fear retirement or lack because You are my shepherd, and I shall not want."

The phrase *"daily bread"* encompasses everything we need for life and godliness. It's not just food on the table—it's resources for every area of life, wisdom for every decision, strength for every challenge.

Relationships—Vertical and Horizontal

The fifth element of the Lord's Prayer deals with relationships: *"Forgive us our debts, as we forgive our debtors."* This is where we get our hearts clean before God (vertical) and clear with others (horizontal).

First, we ask for God's forgiveness. "Father, forgive me for my attitudes, my words, my thoughts that don't honor You. Create in me a clean heart and a right spirit. Let the meditations of my heart be acceptable to You."

Then we extend forgiveness to others. "Lord, I forgive those who have hurt me, stolen from me, lied about me. I release them from my judgment and place them in Your hands. Help me to bless my enemies as my Savior told me to."

Forgiveness isn't just about being nice—it's about being free. Unforgiveness is a prison we build for ourselves. When we forgive others, we're not excusing their behavior; we're releasing ourselves from the burden of carrying their debt.

Forgiveness isn't just about being nice—
it's about being *free*.

Notice that Jesus connected our forgiveness from God with our forgiveness of others. It's not that God withholds forgiveness if we don't forgive—it's that we can't fully receive what we're not willing to give. Forgiveness opens our hearts to experience God's grace in deeper ways.

Spiritual Warfare

The sixth element is spiritual warfare: *"Do not lead us into temptation, but deliver us from the evil one."* This is how we put on the armor of God and take authority over the enemy's attacks.

"Lord, lead me not into temptation. Help me to resist the lust of the flesh, the lust of the eyes, and the pride of life. Give me strength to say no to what's wrong and yes to what's right."

"Deliver me from evil. Deliver my family from the evil one. I put on the whole armor of God—truth, righteousness, peace, faith, salvation, and the Word of God."

"I bind the power of Satan over my life, my family, my finances, my health. I plead the blood of Jesus over everything that belongs to me. I take authority over every demonic attack in the name that is above every name."

This isn't fear-driven praying—it's faith-driven praying. We're not cowering before the enemy; we're taking dominion over him. Jesus gave us authority over all the power of the enemy, and when we exercise that authority in prayer, Heaven backs us up.

Victory Worship

The Lord's Prayer ends where it began—with worship. *"For Yours is the kingdom and the power and the glory forever. Amen."* We don't just go to God asking; we come worshiping. We don't just end with requests; we return to praise.

This final declaration reminds us who's really in charge. Not the government, not the economy, not our circumstances—God is the one with ultimate authority. His Kingdom will endure when every earthly kingdom falls.

"Yours is the power"—not the enemy's power, not our problems' power, but God's power. The same power that raised Jesus from the dead is available to us today.

"Yours is the glory"—not our glory, not human achievement, but God's glory. Everything we receive, everything we accomplish, everything we become is ultimately for His honor and praise.

The Lord's Prayer isn't meant to be recited once every few years in a public gathering—it's meant to be a daily pattern that shapes our entire prayer life. When you pray through this prayer regularly, several things happen.

You develop intimacy with God as your Father. You learn to worship before you ask. You align your heart with God's will. You learn to trust Him for daily provision. You keep your relationships clean through forgiveness. You take authority over spiritual attacks. You remember who's really in charge.

I encourage you to pray through the Lord's Prayer daily, using it as an outline to guide your time with God. Don't just recite the words—pray through each section, applying it to your specific needs and circumstances.

Start with *"Our Father in heaven, hallowed be Your name,"* and spend time worshiping God for who He is. Hallow His name and thank Him for what His name means in your life.

Move to *"Your kingdom come. Your will be done on earth as it is in heaven,"* and pray for your family, your church, your nation, and the lost. Surrender your will to His perfect plan.

Continue with *"Give us this day our daily bread,"* and ask God to meet your practical needs—financial, physical, relational, and spiritual.

Proceed to *"Forgive us our debts, as we forgive our debtors,"* and get your heart clean before God and clear with others.

Follow with *"Do not lead us into temptation, but deliver us from the evil one,"* and put on your spiritual armor for the day.

Finish with *"For Yours is the kingdom and the power and the glory forever,"* returning to worship and declaration of God's sovereignty.

The Lord's Prayer isn't meant to be recited once every few years in a public gathering—it's meant to be *a daily pattern* that shapes our entire prayer life.

This prayer contains everything you need for victorious Christian living. It starts with worship, moves through surrender, asks for provision, maintains right relationships, claims protection, and ends in victory.

When you learn to pray the Lord's Prayer with understanding and faith, you're not just reciting words—you're entering into the very heart of God and accessing everything He has for His children.

The Lord's Prayer isn't just a model—it's a gateway. It's the key that unlocks the treasure house of Heaven and gives us access to all the resources of our Father's Kingdom. When you pray the pattern—delivered to us by the Savior Himself—with faith and expectancy, you're praying one of the most powerful prayers you can pray.

Your Short Prayer:

Father in Heaven, Your Name is holy and glorious and infinitely powerful. I worship You for who You are and thank You that I can come to You as Your child. May Your Kingdom rule saturate my life, my family, and my circumstances. It's Your will, not my own that I want. Give me and my household everything we need to thrive and live for Your glory. Forgive me as I forgive others. Protect me from temptation and deliver me from evil. For Yours is the Kingdom and the power and the glory forever. Amen.

CHAPTER 15

When You Need the Blessings of God's Face

A 32-Word Prayer

And the L*ORD spoke to Moses, saying: "Speak to Aaron and his sons, saying, 'This is the way you shall bless the children of Israel. Say to them:* ***The* L*ORD bless you and keep you; the* L*ORD make His face shine upon you, and be gracious to you; the* L*ORD lift up His countenance upon you, and give you peace.*** *' So they shall put My name on the children of Israel, and I will bless them."*

(NUMBERS 6:22–27)

These ancient words, often called the Aaronic Blessing, may represent the oldest prayer in continuous use in human history. For over 3,400 years, this benediction has been spoken over God's people, carrying with it the promise of heavenly favor, protection, and wholeness.

I believe those words still carry the same power they did back then. Which is why they have been a regular part of my daily and weekly rhythms for a very long time now.

For example, decades ago I co-wrote a song based on the words of that blessing. You may not be aware that I was a musician before I was a pastor. I still love to worship with my saxophone, privately and in corporate worship at the church it is my privilege to pastor.

If you've been around for a while and remember Contemporary Christian music from the '80s and '90s, you almost certainly know the name Phil Driscoll. Decades ago, Phil and I were in a recording studio working on an album and we needed one additional song to close out the project. Phil looked at me and said, "Jentezen, why don't you write one!"

At first I was reluctant, but he wouldn't let me off the hook. He said, "You're both a preacher and musician. You can do this." As it happened, I had just been studying and meditating on the Aaronic Blessing from Numbers six. So with that blessing serving as the basis for the lyrics, we had a wonderful song—"The Lord Bless and Keep Thee"—written in a few hours.

A few years later, when my kids were all small and the littlest of them still in car seats, we used to sing that song as I drove them to school. I couldn't think of better words to sing over them just before I sent them into that school building. And right before driving away, I'd lay hands on them and speak that blessing one more time. It was a normal part of the beginning of each weekday.

Several years ago, speaking this blessing also became a part of our weekly church services. I rarely close a service without speaking those words over our congregation. You're about to understand why.

What makes this prayer extraordinary isn't just its age—it's the fact that when we speak these words, we're not just offering some kind wishes, we're releasing the very name and nature of God into someone's life.

This isn't just a beautiful religious tradition or a poetic way to end a church service. No, this is a God-given supernatural weapon against every curse. A divine antidote to every fear. And a heavenly insurance policy against every attack of the enemy.

When you understand the power contained in these simple phrases, you'll never again underestimate the impact of a biblical blessing.

> **This is a God-given *supernatural weapon* against every curse.**

If you need God's favor to shine upon your circumstances, if you need His protection over your family, if you need His peace in your heart—this ancient blessing holds keys that can unlock Heaven's storehouse over your life.

To understand the power of the Aaronic Blessing, we need to understand its origin. Neither Moses nor Aaron came up with these words. In Numbers 6:22, God clearly chose the phrasing for this blessing. These are words from Him.

Please understand, God didn't give this blessing as a suggestion or a nice religious custom. He gave it as a specific instruction to Moses, who was to teach it to Aaron and his sons—the priests of Israel.

Notice the precise wording: *"This is the way you shall bless the children of Israel."* Not "this is *a* way" or "here's an option." No, this is *the* way. God was establishing the official method by which His people would be blessed, and He wanted it done exactly as He prescribed.

But here's what makes this blessing unique: God promises that when these words are spoken over His people, something supernatural happens:

> *"So they shall put My name on the children of Israel, and I will bless them."* (v. 27)

When the Aaronic Blessing is pronounced, God's own name is placed upon the person or people being blessed, and God Himself promises to personally back up that blessing with His power.

This means that when you speak these words over someone in faith—or when someone speaks them over you and you receive them in faith—you're not just offering good wishes. You're literally putting the name of Almighty God upon that person, and God declares, *"I will bless them."*

This sacred blessing has three distinct sections. If the blessing was a song, we'd say there are three "bars" or "stanzas." Each of these stanzas builds upon the previous one, building to a thrilling finish of favor. Let's explore each of them.

First Stanza: The Lord Bless You and Keep You.

The blessing opens with powerful authority:

> *"The Lord bless you and keep you."* (v. 24)

If that was all this blessing contained—if it ended right there—it would still be the best words that could ever be spoken over you. Why? Because the Hebrew word for "bless" here is *barak* (בָּרַךְ), which means to bend down, to show favor, to enrich, to prosper. When God *blesses* someone, He's not just wishing them well—He's bending low to meet them where they are and enrich their lives in every way possible.

But notice the declaration moves on from "bless" and also says, "keep." The word translated "keep" there is the Hebrew *shamar* (שָׁמַר), which means to guard, to protect, to watch over, to preserve. It's the same word used to describe a shepherd watching over his flock or a guard protecting a treasure.

This reveals something beautiful about God's heart: He doesn't just bless us and walk away. He blesses us and then guards those blessings. He enriches our lives and then protects what He's given us. He prospers us and then watches over that prosperity to ensure the enemy can't steal it.

> **When God *blesses* someone, He's not just wishing them well—He's bending low to meet them where they are and enrich their lives in every way possible.**

How many times have you received a blessing only to lose it shortly afterward? How many times has an exciting open door of opportunity been slammed shut by circumstances? The Aaronic Blessing addresses this by combining blessing with keeping; favor with protection; and prosperity with preservation.

Second Stanza: The Lord Make His Face Shine Upon You, and Be Gracious to You.

The second bar of this song takes the blessing to even higher levels:

> *"The Lord make His face shine upon you,*
> *and be gracious to you."* (v. 25)

The term "face" here is so very significant. It tells us that this is clearly about more than material blessings—this is about relationship, acceptance, and divine favor.

This idea of seeing the king's face meant much more to people in ancient Middle Eastern cultures than it does for us today. At that time most people lived and died without ever once catching a glimpse of their king's face. And even fewer had the experience of knowing that the king had seen *them*. And fewer still ever had an experience in which they knew the king had not only seen them but had actually smiled or shown approval when he looked at them.

When a king's face "shined" upon someone, it meant they had found favor in his sight. That he was pleased with them. It meant they were welcomed into his presence, accepted in his court, and given access to his resources. And when someone fell out of favor, the king would "hide his face" from them, cutting off access and relationship.

When a king's face "shined" upon someone, it meant they had *found favor* in his sight. That he was pleased with them.

With that in mind, now think about the implications of having a spokesman for God, a priest of the Most High, pronounce these words over you. "*The LORD make His face shine upon you...*" (v. 25). It would be mind-blowing and wonderful beyond description. And yet those are the exact words God gave the sons of Aaron to speak over God's people.

Today, in the new covenant, every believer is a priest of the Most High God (1 Peter 2:9; Revelation 1:6). So, we can pronounce this blessing, too! When we pray for God's face to shine upon someone, we're asking for them to experience divine acceptance, heavenly approval, and unlimited access to the throne room of grace. We're praying that they would never have to wonder if God is pleased with them or if they're welcome in His presence.

Following the words about God's shining face, we see the phrase "... *and be gracious to you*" (v. 25). This adds another sweet layer of meaning. The root of the word "gracious" is *grace*. And grace isn't just "unmerited favor"—it's God's supernatural ability working in you to do what you cannot do in your own strength. When God is gracious to you, He doesn't just forgive your failures; He empowers you to succeed where you've previously failed. What a wonderful thought. Yet it just keeps getting better.

Third Stanza: The Lord Lift Up His Countenance Upon You, and Give You Peace.

The final bars of this gospel song bring the blessing to its climax:

> *"The* Lord *lift up His countenance upon you,*
> *and give you peace."* (v. 26)

The word "countenance" refers, again, to God's face, but in a different sense than the previous line. Here, it's about God's intense, personal attention and care. In other words, before we were talking about a *king's* face. But now we're talking about our heavenly *Father's* face.

When God lifts up His countenance upon you, He's giving you His undivided attention. He's focusing His infinite love, wisdom, and power on your specific situation. It's the picture of a loving father who stops everything else he's doing to give his full attention to his child.

And the result of this divine attention? "Peace." Not just the absence of conflict, but the Hebrew *shalom* (שָׁלוֹם)—wholeness, completeness, everything in perfect order and harmony. This is peace that passes understanding, peace in the storm, peace that guards your heart and mind.

Yet the most amazing thing about the Aaronic Blessing is found in God's promise that follows it:

"So they shall put My name on the children of Israel, and I will bless them." (v. 27)

When this full blessing is spoken, something supernatural happens—God's name is literally placed upon the person being blessed.

In biblical times, a name represented far more than just identification. A name carried authority, power, and character. When you carried someone's name, you carried their authority and had access to their resources.

Think about what it means to carry God's name. It means you carry His authority over every demonic force. It means you have access to His unlimited resources. It means His character—His love, wisdom, power, and faithfulness—becomes available to you in every situation.

When this blessing is spoken over you, you don't just receive good wishes. You receive the name that is above every name. The name that causes demons to tremble. The name that opens doors no man can shut. The name that brings healing to the sick and freedom to the captives.

We need to become people who speak blessing in a cursed world. God's Word declares that the power of life and death are in the tongue (Proverbs 18:21). We live in a world that specializes in speaking curses. Turn on the news and you'll hear predictions of doom, declarations of failure, and proclamations of defeat. Social media is filled with negative words, critical spirits, and destructive speech.

Even well-meaning people often speak more curses than blessings without realizing it. Far too often, we speak curses over and upon *ourselves*!

But God's people are called to be different. First Peter 2:9 says, *"But ye are a chosen generation, a royal priesthood, an holy nation, a peculiar people; that ye should shew forth the praises of him who hath called you out of darkness into his marvellous light"* (KJV). It tells us we're priests and also says we are a peculiar people! What could be more peculiar than to be blessers in a world filled with cursers? To speak life in a culture of death? To release favor where others release fear?

This blessing gives us a powerful tool for doing exactly that. Instead of agreeing with the negative reports, we can speak God's blessing. Instead of rehearsing the problems, we can declare God's promises. Instead of joining the chorus of complaint, we can lift our voices in blessing.

Instead of rehearsing the problems, we can *declare* God's promises.

This isn't just about being positive—it's about being *biblical*. It's about partnering with Heaven's agenda rather than Hell's strategy. It's about releasing the creative power of God's Word instead of the destructive power of negative confession.

While the Aaronic Blessing was originally given for priests to speak over the people of Israel, because of the gospel and what Jesus accomplished, we can apply these principles in our personal lives (Ephesians 3:6). Here are several ways to make this ancient blessing a powerful part of your spiritual arsenal:

1. Blessing Your Family

Start each day by speaking the Aaronic Blessing over your spouse and children. Place your hands on them if possible and declare: "The Lord bless you and keep you; the Lord make His face shine upon you and be gracious to you; the Lord lift up His countenance upon you and give you peace."

Watch what happens when you make this a consistent practice. Your family relationships will improve. Your children will walk with greater confidence. Your spouse will experience more of God's favor.

Why? Because you're putting God's name on them daily and releasing His blessing in their lives.

2. Blessing Your Circumstances

You can also speak this blessing over your specific situations. Facing a business challenge? Declare God's blessing and keeping power over your work. Dealing with health issues? Ask God to make His face shine upon your body and be gracious to your healing. Struggling with relationships? Pray for God's peace to reign in those connections.

3. Blessing Others

Look for opportunities to speak blessing over other people. Instead of joining in gossip or criticism, speak words that release God's favor. When someone shares a struggle, respond with blessing rather than sympathy. When you see someone succeeding, speak additional blessing over their efforts.

Here's the most encouraging part of the entire passage: after giving the exact words of blessing the priests were to speak, God makes a personal promise: "*... and I will bless them*" (v. 27).

Look for opportunities to *speak blessing* over other people.

Isn't that glorious? God adds His personal assurance that He will honor the words of this blessing. God is faithful. He watches over His Word to perform it (Jeremiah 1:12). In fact, later on in this same book of Numbers we find these words:

> *"God is not a man, that He should lie,*

Nor a son of man, that He should repent.
Has He said, and will He not do?
Or has He spoken, and will He not make it good?"
(Numbers 23:19)

God's promise isn't dependent on the eloquence of the person speaking the blessing or the worthiness of the person receiving it. When the blessing is spoken according to God's pattern, God Himself takes responsibility for bringing it to pass.

This should give us tremendous confidence in speaking blessing over others. We're not trying to manipulate God or twist His arm. We're simply coming into alignment with His desire to bless His people. We're receiving what He already wants to do.

It also means that when someone speaks this blessing over you, you can receive it with faith, knowing that God Himself is backing up those words with His power and authority.

Yes, by speaking this blessing over your household and others, you're carrying on a holy tradition that began in the Wilderness of Sinai thirty-five centuries ago.

In fact, archaeological discoveries have confirmed just how seriously the ancient Israelites took this blessing. In 1979, archaeologists discovered two small silver amulets in a tomb near Jerusalem, dating back to around 600 BC.[4] Inscribed on these tiny scrolls were portions of the Aaronic Blessing, making them the earliest surviving biblical texts ever discovered.

This means that over 2,600 years ago, people were carrying these words with them as a prompt and a reminder. They understood that these weren't just ceremonial words—they were declarations of divine favor that could make a practical difference in their daily lives.

Today, thousands of years later, these same words carry the same power. When spoken in faith, they still release God's favor, protection, and peace. They still put God's name on people. They still move Heaven to respond with blessing.

This is why I speak this blessing over the congregation of the church I pastor almost every time we gather. And why, even before I began that practice, I had been speaking it over my children daily, from the time they were very small.

Hopefully, that tells you how much I believe in the power of declaring these ancient, holy words in faith.

One of the most beautiful aspects of the Aaronic Blessing is that it tends to multiply and "boomerang." When you begin speaking blessing over others, you often find that blessing returns to you in greater measure.

You see, God is a *blesser* by nature. His desire is to pour out good things on His children. When we partner with Him in that desire by speaking blessing over others, we align ourselves with His purposes and open ourselves up to receive more of His favor in return.

This creates a beautiful cycle: the more we bless, the more blessed we become. The more we speak favor over others, the more favor we experience in our own lives. The more we release God's peace into other people's circumstances, the more His peace guards our own hearts.

This ancient blessing contains everything you need for a life of divine favor and supernatural peace. When you learn to speak these words with faith and understanding, you're not just reciting a beautiful prayer—you're releasing the power of God's name and His blessing over every situation you face.

This creates a beautiful cycle: the more we bless, the more *blessed* we become.

Today, whatever challenge you're confronting, whatever fear is trying to grip your heart, whatever area of your life needs God's touch—remember that you have access to the most powerful blessing ever given. You can place God's name upon your circumstances and watch Him respond with favor that defies human explanation and peace that passes all understanding.

The same God who gave this blessing to Moses all those centuries ago is ready to fulfill it in your life today. Look up; His face is shining upon you.

Your Short Prayer for Yourself:

Lord, may You bless and keep me.
May You make Your face shine upon me and
be gracious to me. Lord, lift up Your Fatherly
countenance upon me, and give me peace.
I receive Your blessing, Your protection,
Your favor, and Your peace. Your name be
upon my life and my house.

Your Short Prayer for Others:

The Lord bless you and keep you; the Lord make His face shine upon you and be gracious to you; the Lord lift up His countenance upon you and give you peace. May you receive His blessing, His protection, His favor, and His peace. May His holy name be glorified in all that concerns you.

ACKNOWLEDGEMENTS

A special thank you to my wife Cherise, whose endless love and inspiration lift me up every day. To my children and grandchildren, you are a profound blessing and a constant source of joy in my life.

I want to say a huge thank you to Tracy Page, Jason Vernon, Natasha Phillips and Brian Smith! Your encouragement through the process of writing this book, and your support for the ministry means the world.

To Terry Redmon, Brooke Loftis, and the exceptional teams at Breakfast for Seven and Inprov, I am immensely grateful for your partnership in bringing this book to life.

David Holland, your extraordinary support and talent have been the driving force behind this book and I am so grateful for your help in bringing this message to readers around the world.

Finally, to my congregation at Free Chapel and our partners at Jentezen Franklin Media Ministries, thank you for your love and support. Together, we continue to share the gospel, touching hearts and changing lives for the glory of God.

APPENDIX

Other Short Prayers of the Bible

When You Need Supernatural Revelation

Daniel 12:8 (10 words)

Although I heard, I did not understand. Then I said, ***"My lord, what shall be the end of these things?"***

When You Want God to Bless Your Work or Efforts

Psalm 90:17 (27 words)

Let the beauty of the LORD our God be upon us, and establish the work of our hands for us; yes, establish the work of our hands.

When You Don't Know What to Do

Acts 9:6 (8 words)

So [Paul], trembling and astonished, said, ***"Lord, what do You want me to do?"*** *Then the Lord said to him, "Arise and go into the city, and you will be told what you must do."*

When You Need Wisdom

1 Kings 3:7–9 (31 words)

"Now, O Lord my God, You have made Your servant king instead of my father David, but I am a little child; I do not know how to go out or come in. And Your servant is in the midst of Your people whom You have chosen, a great people, too numerous to be numbered or counted. ***Therefore give to Your servant an understanding heart to judge Your people, that I may discern between good and evil. For who is able to judge this great people of Yours?"***

When You Need God to Show Up in Power

1 Kings 18:36–37 (64 words)

And it came to pass, at the time of the offering of the evening sacrifice, that Elijah the prophet came near and said, ***"Lord God of Abraham, Isaac, and Israel, let it be known this day that You are God in Israel and I am Your servant, and that I have done all these things at Your word. Hear me, O Lord, hear me, that this people may know that You are the Lord God, and that You have turned their hearts back to You again."***

When You Are Under Attack

2 Chronicles 14:11 (51 words)

And Asa cried out to the LORD his God, and said, ***"LORD, it is nothing for You to help, whether with many or with those who have no power; help us, O LORD our God, for we rest on You, and in Your name we go against this multitude. O LORD, You are our God; do not let man prevail against You!"***

When You Want to Express Thankfulness to God

Psalm 75:1, ESV (20 words)

We give thanks to you, O God; we give thanks, for your name is near. We recount your wondrous deeds.

When You Feel Weak in Faith

Mark 9:23–24 (6 words)

Jesus said to him, "If you can believe, all things are possible to him who believes." Immediately the father of the child cried out and said with tears, ***"Lord, I believe; help my unbelief!"***

When You Need Mercy

Luke 18:13 (7 words)

"And the tax collector, standing afar off, would not so much as raise his eyes to heaven, but beat his breast, saying, ***'God, be merciful to me a sinner!'"***

When You Need Forgiveness

Psalm 51:10–12 (47 words)

Create in me a clean heart, O God, and renew a steadfast spirit within me. Do not cast me away from Your presence, and do not take Your Holy Spirit from me. Restore to me the joy of Your salvation, and uphold me by Your generous Spirit.

When You Need Boldness in Your Witness

Acts 4:29–31 (43 words)

"Now, Lord, look on their threats, and grant to Your servants that with all boldness they may speak Your word, by stretching out Your hand to heal, and that signs and wonders may be done through the name of Your holy Servant Jesus." And when they had prayed, the place where they were assembled together was shaken; and they were all filled with the Holy Spirit, and they spoke the word of God with boldness.

ENDNOTES

[1] Spurgeon, Charles Haddon. *Spurgeon at His Best: Over 2200 Striking Quotations from the World's Most Exhaustive and Widely-read Sermon Series.* Compiled by Tom Carter. Grand Rapids, MI: Baker Publishing Group, 1988, 126.

[2] Albert B. Simpson, *Hymns of the Christian Life* (1910).

[3] Bill Gaither, *"He Touched Me"* (1964).

[4] The Israel Museum, Jerusalem, *"'Priestly Benediction' on Amulets,"* The Israel Museum, Jerusalem, https://www.imj.org.il/en/collections/198069-0.

Jentezen Franklin Media Ministries aims to be a source of help and hope around the world. From comforting God's people in Israel, protecting the unborn, feeding the hungry, supporting hurting families, providing relief in areas struck by a natural disaster, to broadcasting the gospel—our mission is to share God's love and champion Jesus Christ to the nations!

STAY CONNECTED:

JOIN US LIVE ON TV:

For broadcasting times and channel listings, go to:

JENTEZENFRANKLIN.ORG/TV-SCHEDULE

To donate and learn more about the outreaches of Jentezen Franklin Media Ministries, go to:

JENTEZENFRANKLIN.ORG/OUTREACH